T0328477

Cambridge Elements ≡

Elements in Child Development
edited by
Marc H. Bornstein
National Institute of Child Health and Human Development, Bethesda
Institute for Fiscal Studies, London
UNICEF, New York City

CHILD WELFARE, PROTECTION, AND JUSTICE

Murli Desai

Tata Institute of Social Sciences
National University of Singapore and Seoul National University

CAMBRIDGE
UNIVERSITY PRESS

CAMBRIDGE
UNIVERSITY PRESS

University Printing House, Cambridge CB2 8BS, United Kingdom

One Liberty Plaza, 20th Floor, New York, NY 10006, USA

477 Williamstown Road, Port Melbourne, VIC 3207, Australia

314–321, 3rd Floor, Plot 3, Splendor Forum, Jasola District Centre, New Delhi – 110025, India

79 Anson Road, #06–04/06, Singapore 079906

Cambridge University Press is part of the University of Cambridge.

It furthers the University's mission by disseminating knowledge in the pursuit of education, learning, and research at the highest international levels of excellence.

www.cambridge.org
Information on this title: www.cambridge.org/9781108965637
DOI: 10.1017/9781108963787

© Murli Desai 2021

First published 2021

A catalogue record for this publication is available from the British Library.

ISBN 978-1-108-96563-7 Paperback
ISSN 2632-9948 (online)
ISSN 2632-993X (print)

Child Welfare, Protection, and Justice

Elements in Child Development

DOI: 10.1017/9781108963787
First published online: January 2021

Murli Desai
Tata Institute of Social Sciences
National University of Singapore and Seoul National University
Author for correspondence: Murli Desai, murlidesai@gmail.com

Abstract: This Element first reviews the limitations of the concepts of problems in childhood. It proposes a universal, comprehensive, and longitudinal conceptual framework of problems in childhood, their differential context, and their cyclical effects. Based on the linkages identified in the children's problems, they are divided into three levels: primary, secondary, and tertiary. The Element then reviews the concepts and the limitations of the prevalent service delivery approaches of child welfare, protection, and justice, because of which these services have not helped to break the cycle of problems in childhood. The Element identifies the rights-based comprehensive, preventive, and systemic approach for child welfare, at primary, secondary, and tertiary prevention levels, in order to break this cycle of problems. Finally, the Element goes into details of tertiary-prevention-level integrated service delivery for children facing sociolegal problems.

Keywords: child welfare, child protection, justice for children, preventive service delivery systems, child rights

Isbns: 9781108965637 (PB), 9781108963787 (OC)
Issns: 2632-9948 (online), 2632-993X (print)

Contents

1 Scope of the Element   1

2 Conceptual Framework of Problems in Childhood   1

3 Conceptual Framework of Service Delivery Systems for
  Child Welfare   26

4 Service Delivery Systems for Children with Sociolegal
  Problems   52

References   73

1 Scope of the Element

This Element starts with a review of concepts of problems in childhood. It examines the need for specific and universal concepts as well as the need for contextualising and linking of problems in childhood. In order to identify the common causal factors of problems in childhood, it first discusses the social construction of childhood with reference to adultism, sexism, schooling, and Western development sciences, and the extension of childhood to include adolescence. It then discusses the implications of industrialisation and global-isation for childhood. The Element proposes a universal comprehensive and longitudinal conceptual framework of problems in childhood, their differential context, and their cyclical effects. Based on the linkages identified in the children's problems, they are divided into three consecutive levels: primary, secondary, and tertiary.

The Element then reviews the concepts and the service delivery approaches of child welfare, protection, and justice with reference to their limitations, because of which these services have not helped to break the cycle of problems in childhood. The Element identifies a child rights–based, comprehensive, preventive, and systemic conceptual framework of service delivery systems for child welfare through Family Service Centres. This framework helps to develop service delivery for children at primary, secondary, and tertiary pre-vention levels in order to break this cycle of problems at these levels.

Finally, the Element details the tertiary-prevention-levels integrated service delivery systems in four categories. These include integrated alternative child-care services for children without parental care, integrated child protection services for child victims of violence, integrated child welfare services for children in emergencies, and integrated child reintegration services for children in conflict with law and those associated with armed conflict.

2 Conceptual Framework of Problems in Childhood

2.1 Overview

This section starts with a review of the need for specific and universal concepts as well as the need for contextualising and linking problems in childhood. In order to identify the common causal factors of problems in childhood, it first discusses the social construction of childhood with reference to adultism, sexism, schooling, and Western development sciences, and the extension of childhood to include adolescence. It then discusses the implications of industri-alisation and globalisation for childhood. Finally, The Element proposes a universal comprehensive and longitudinal conceptual framework of problems in childhood, their differential contexts, and their cyclical effects. Based on the linkages identified, the problems are conceptually divided into three consecutive levels: primary, secondary, and tertiary.

2.2 Review of Concepts of Problems in Childhood

2.2.1 Need for Specific and Universal Concepts of Problems in Childhood

In Western countries, the discussion on children's problems started with a focus on poverty and crime among children. Beginning around 1825, it became gradually recognised in the United States that public authorities had a duty to intervene in these cases, the cause of which was identified as parental neglect. The first juvenile court was set up in Chicago in 1899, with the understanding that there should be no real distinctions between neglected children, then legally classified as 'dependent', and child offenders if society was to achieve a realistic approach to crime prevention. In the mid-twentieth century, modern X-ray technology provided new documentation of physical abuse of children at home that forced a reappraisal of society's responsibility to protect children, even from their own parents. The child protection movement began in the United States where child abuse was added to child neglect, both of which require protection of children from parents (Thomas Jr, 1972).

For a long time now, the trend in the Western countries has been to use the terms 'child abuse' and 'child neglect' together in knowledge development, laws, and child protection programmes. Today, the International Society for Prevention of Child Abuse and Neglect publishes an international journal called *Child Abuse and Neglect*. The US Federal Child Abuse Prevention and Treatment Act (CAPTA), as amended and reauthorised by the CAPTA Reauthorization Act of 2010, defines child abuse and neglect as, at a minimum, 'any recent act or failure to act on the part of a parent or caretaker which results in death, serious physical or emotional harm, sexual abuse or exploitation (including sexual abuse), or an act or failure to act which presents an imminent risk of serious harm' (cited by Child Welfare Information Gateway, 2019).

Child neglect was rightly linked to poverty. However, poverty may not be the parents' fault. Neglected children, especially in countries with high levels of poverty, need childcare or welfare and not necessarily legal recourse in the same sense that child victims of abuse need. The concepts and services for the two, therefore, need to be separated and made more appropriate.

Because of the greater prevalence of child abuse but less commercial exploitation in Western countries, not only is commercial exploitation of children neglected in Western books, some Western authors use the term 'child abuse' to include commercial exploitation of children, even when they examine child abuse across the globe (e.g., Schwartz-Kenney, McCauley, & Epstein, 2000). The World Health Organization (WHO, 2020) uses the term 'child maltreatment' to include abuse and neglect of children. Thus, neglect, abuse, maltreatment, and exploitation are often used synonymously, and the terms do overlap. However, the terms need to be distinguished and made specific. Child neglect, abuse, and exploitation are significantly different, with different causes, as discussed later in this Element. Therefore, strategies to prevent and address them will also have to be different.

2.2.2 Need for Contextualising and Linking Problems in Childhood

Because Western literature focuses on child abuse and neglect, the literature on child protection in developing countries often lists problems faced by children. The explanation for this can be found in the history of the United Nations Children's Fund (UNICEF)'s with reference to child protection. Until the mid 1980s, UNICEF focused its work around the world on children's basic needs of education and health. In 1986, it carried out a policy review of 'children in especially difficult circumstances' that included abandoned children, street children, child victims of abuse and neglect, and children in armed conflict, and one year later, child labour (UNICEF, 2006). It used this list of problems of children in developing countries. However, mere listing results in children being labelled neglected, socially handicapped, deficient, illegitimate, delinquent, a street child, child labourer, trafficked child, child prostitute, and so on, focuses only on manifestations of the problems. A consequence of such symptoms-based targeting is labelling which leads to reduction of people's whole life stories to a specific problem. People are often labeled in ways that convey misinterpretations of an underlying problem. Labels stigmatise children. Moreover, people may use labels to gain privileged access to resources. Although labels are used to indicate diversity, they may homogenise people into stereotypes (Power of Labelling, 2006). The response to labelling has been development of separate schemes of services for each 'category' of children. Such a scheme approach has led to fragmentation of service delivery that addresses only symptoms, although most problems have common causes. As a result, causes of the problems have remained untouched.

Children and their problems do not exist in isolation; there are linkages among problems faced by children, with common causes, in the context of family and community. These linkages are necessary in order to understand the cycle of problems as well as the differential contexts, manifestations, and consequences in each problem situation to help prioritise preventative services.

A conceptual framework is proposed here to deconstruct problems in childhood. That framework is universal, comprehensive, and longitudinal.

2.3 Social Construction of Childhood and Adolescence

2.3.1 Introduction to Social Construction of Childhood

To identify the common causal factors of problems in childhood, this section first discusses the social construction of childhood. According to Aries (1962, cited from James & James, 2004), childhood did not exist in medieval society, as younger members of society were not granted special or distinctive social status. They participated in society according to their abilities, just as adults did. Jans (2004) noted that until the eighteenth century, children were protected and cherished till they were six or seven years old, after which they were considered pocket-sized adults, mostly involved in employment. Industrial capitalism has led to science, policies, and programmes that shaped the social construction of childhood. According to the sociological paradigm, childhood is neither a natural nor a universal feature of human groups. It is a variable which can never be entirely divorced from other variables such as class, gender, or ethnicity (Prout & James, 1997, cited in Gallacher & Kehily, 2013). Biology does not determine childhood or adolescence, but provides a context for it, just as biology (sex) does not determine but provides the context for the gendered lives of girls and women.

The prejudicing ideologies such as adultism, sexism, ableism, racism, casteism, etc., justify role stereotypes, and therefore create social constructions of hierarchy, exclusion, domination, intolerance, oppression, exploitation, and violence against all children, and more so among girls, children with disability, children from marginalised ethnicities/castes/indigenous people/tribes, etc. This section focuses on social construction of childhood created by adultism and sexism.

2.3.2 Social Construction of Childhood by Adultism

According to Le Francois (2013), adultism is understood as the oppression experienced by children and young people at the hands of adults and adult-produced/adult-tailored systems. It relates to sociopolitical status differentials and power relations endemic to adult–child relationships. Adultism may include experiences of individual prejudice, discrimination, violence, and abuse, as well as social control and systemic oppression. At an individual level, it is characterised by adult authoritarianism towards children and adult-centric perspectives in interacting with children and in understanding children's experiences. Systemic adultism is characterised by adult-centric legislation, policies, rules, and practices that are embedded within social structures and institutions which impact negatively on children's daily lives and result in disadvantage and oppressive social relationships.

Patriarchal families are adultist, where children are supposed to be obedient to elders and have little say in decisions which are made for them. Patriarchy developed as a system of control and distribution of resources by hierarchies of age, gender, and generation, leading to strict determination of roles and responsibilities. The father or the eldest male is considered the patriarch or 'head of the household'. Control over resources and assumption of superiority give the patriarch the power to make decisions about his dependents, which mainly include women and children. If a child asserts himself or herself, in the process of disagreeing with the elder or making his or her own life choices, the family's unity and stability are perceived to be threatened. Thus, children are made vulnerable to subordination and control in such families.

White (2003) emphasised that, because children and young people are of course vulnerable and in need of adult protection in some senses and situations, approaches to analysis or action that focus on vulnerability alone are problematic. They are likely to encourage notions of the young as passive, helpless victims, obscuring their strengths and competences, their own ideas about ways of coping with adversity, and their rights to take part as active agents in their own development. James and James (2004) noted that adult control over children is often justified as necessary for their welfare. However, adult control is often a means to maintain conformity and social order between the generations as adults seek to preserve and recreate the childhood they remember. Children are known to have agency by birth; however, the life-cycle approach is useful to understanding the evolving capacities of children, and the need to balance dependency and autonomy across the stages of early and middle childhood and adolescence, broadly covering zero to six years, six to twelve years, and twelve to eighteen years, respectively.

According to the EU Canada Project (2003), adultism may lead to protective exclusion in the following ways: withholding information and access to entitlements on the basis that children are too immature or incapable of using them 'properly'; acting 'on behalf of a child or young person' using the same rationale; making decisions about a child or young person based on generalised representations of children and young people rather than consulting with or treating situations on their individual merits; and acting as a barrier to the autonomy, independence, and empowerment of children and young people individually or collectively. Moreover, when adults are given the authority to control children under their care by disciplining them, child abuse comes to be institutionalised in the family, schools, and society. Thus, from an adultist perspective, child abuse is not an anomaly, but it is built into the way in which childhood is defined.

2.3.3 Social Construction of Female Childhood by Sexism

Sexism implies stereotypes of women's physical and mental capabilities, which have led to role stereotypes of earner for men and housewife for women, headship for men and subordination for women and, therefore, discrimination against women. Sexism consists of attitudes, policies, institutional structures, and actions that discriminate against one sex (often but not always, against women), limiting freedom and opportunities (Griffin, 2008).

'Sex' refers to the biological differences between male and female: the visible difference in genitalia, and the related difference in procreative function (Connelly et al., 2000). For ages, it was believed that the different characteristics, roles, and statuses accorded to women and men in society were determined by biology (that is, sex), that they were natural and, therefore, not changeable. The distinction between sex and gender was introduced to deal with this tendency to attribute women's subordination to their anatomy. Gender is a matter of culture; it refers to the social classification of men and women into 'masculine' and 'feminine'. Gender has no biological origin; the connections between sex and gender are not natural (Bhasin, 2000).

From a very early age, children learn their gender roles and societal expectations from them, along with their respective future social, productive, and reproductive roles. Girls are often trained as passive, submissive, and emotional human beings, whereas in most cultures boys and men are expected to be physically strong and sexually successful, to be risk-takers and decision-makers, and to provide financially for their wives and children. Such socialisation leads to discrimination against girls from childhood with reference to education, health, and other social services. Boys are socialised into a sense of superiority over girls and this may cause some boys to be aggressive towards girls, and most girls are socialised to be submissive and tolerant of this violence (Save the Children, 2009).

2.3.4 Social Construction of Dependency in Middle Childhood by Schooling

The eighteenth-century philosopher Rousseau is credited with inventing the modern notion of childhood as a distinct period of human life with needs of stimulation and education. There was an outrage over the conditions of child labourers in factories in the West in the late eighteenth century, which had less to do with exploitation of the child labourers than with fears of their unruly and potentially undesirable activities made possible by an independent income

(Burman, 2008). Ruddick (2003) noted that the modern childhood and youth that emerged at the turn of the nineteenth century in industrialising nations also had strong links to the anxieties of a growing middle class in those countries about their children's future. For this class, the rise of industrial capitalism required a shift in strategies of social reproduction towards an increasingly educated (male) progeny, as the paths into clerical and managerial work. These paths were directed increasingly through the classroom and away from the 'shop floor'. Such a shift from child labour work to clerical work required schooling, especially in middle childhood.

Middle childhood was thus constructed through schooling, justifying making children dependent and imposing a middle-class ideal of childhood as a period of helplessness (Hendrick, 1990, cited in Burman, 2008). This model of childhood upheld the innocence of children. Childhood thus emerged as a domain to be colonised and civilised (Burman, 2008). Education took children away from work to schools. As families detached from kinship communities, children became the focal point for parents' gaze. Both school and family now acted as disciplinary structures through which children were domesticated (Wyness, 2012). Due to schooling (and family), the position of children evolved from strong social participation with minimal protection during the eighteenth and nineteenth centuries to strong protection with minimal participation during the twentieth century (Jans, 2004). Separation was realised between environments of children and adults. As a result, children came to spend most of their time among themselves, secluded from the rest of society, in a psychosocial moratorium (Dasberg, 1965, cited in Jans, 2004).

2.3.5 Social Construction of 'Normal' Childhood by Western Development Sciences

Developmental psychology has contributed significantly to understanding childhood in its various stages; however, developmentalism and its 'ages and stages' model of childhood based on biology, has several implications. Boyden and Levison (2000) noted that the overall trend in developmental science accepts transformation from immature child to mature adult, simple to complex, irrational to rational behaviours, and dependent childhood to autonomous adulthood. Children are thus understood to be immature beings in a state of development and training for competent adulthood. The concept of 'developing' children into adults by 'teaching' them implies that children are not developed or are incomplete and adults are 'developed' or 'complete' (Levison, 2000).

The Western standards of 'normal' childhood are based on 'adultist' notions of childhood as a basically biologically driven 'natural' phenomenon in which children are distinguished from adults by specific physical and mental (as opposed to social) characteristics. In this 'normal' childhood, children are seen as separated from the world of work and devoting their time to learning and play and thus economically worthless, apolitical, and asexual (White, 2003).

Although children all over the world worked before the advent of formal education, according to most economic models, children are perceived both as a cost to society and as the passive receptacles of benefits and knowledge imparted by adults. In other words, children's integration into society is portrayed, in effect, as a one-way process in which adults give and children receive (Boyden & Levison, 2000). As Wyness, Harrison, and Buchanan (2004) noted, a political community has an exclusive adult membership with children not considered competent for entry. Children's apolitical nature is associated with family being considered their primary social environment, which is seen as the personal and private sphere, shielding children from the public sphere of politics.

Developmentalism has also led to universal chronologisation, based on Western, white, middle class, male constructs of 'normality'. It has institutionalised chronological age within the life course; age is now key to the definition of what a child is. The ways in which developmental science has used age to chart children's development is problematic as not all children achieve the same stages at the same age (James & James, 2012). In different cultures, the movement of individual children through childhood is not followed with much precision, and age is frequently treated as only an approximate benchmark. Many different kinds of criteria – although seldom age – are used to demarcate childhood (Boyden & Levison, 2000). Sigelman and Rider (2006) noted that age means different things in different societies. Each society has its own ways of dividing the life span and of treating the individuals who fall into different age groups. Each socially defined age group in a society is assigned different statuses, roles, privileges, and responsibilities.

2.3.6 Social Construction of Adolescence as an Extension of Childhood

The 'age of majority' is the legal age at which an individual is recognised by a nation as an adult and is expected to meet all obligations attendant to that status, such as voting, marriage, military participation, property ownership, and responsible alcohol consumption. Below the age of majority, an individual is still considered a 'minor'. There is a wide variation in national laws setting minimum age thresholds for participation in these activities. In many countries, the age of majority is eighteen, which is consonant with the upper threshold of the age range for children under the United Nations (UN) Convention on the Rights of the Child (UNCRC, 1989).

Adolescence originated in the late nineteenth-century United States when the need for advanced education produced a greater economic dependence on parents between puberty and the time when an individual achieved economic and social independence. Education introduced two important factors: delay in achieving economic self-sufficiency and social experiences separated from adult life (Lesser & Pope, 2007).

As adolescence is a social construct, its age group differs widely between cultures and social classes. Even though physical maturation may be completed by the age of eighteen years, there can exist much variation in the ages at which children functionally become adults in a society by assuming adult roles and responsibilities. These criteria include the commencement of work, end of schooling, betrothal and marriage, among others. Normally, the criteria that are applied differ according to gender and class. For street or working children, or girls married off in their mid-teens, adolescence may end even earlier. By contrast, during the early years of adulthood, the tasks of adulthood may not yet be completed for those going through advanced education. Thus, it is essential to bear in mind that experiences of adolescence can differ considerably, as a result of differences in socio-economic class and cultural practices; rural, urban, or semi-urban environment; involvement in the labour force instead of the formal educational system, and so on (Boyden & Levison, 2000). Jones (2009) rightly noted that youth is a middle-class phenomenon, a luxury to which the poor have no access as they need to start earning early in life.

Chronologisation has created an artificial dichotomy between childhood and adulthood, as though the two are distinctly different from one another. The distinction between childhood and adulthood at the age of eighteen is arbitrary, fixed first by the sciences and then the UNCRC, negating childhood as a social construct. The prevalent adultist perspective of childhood considers children dependent, incomplete, changing, ignorant, becoming, and therefore rendered powerless; and, by contrast, adults as independent, complete, stable, knowledgeable, being, and therefore given power over the other, alienating one from the other. The former is given rights, and the latter is given duties to protect these rights. In fact, as James and James (2004) emphasised, it is the supposed differences between children and adults that underpin the institution of childhood. Such discontinuities between childhood and adulthood raise the need for and problems with reference to age verification, as two different sets of norms and laws apply to those below and those above the age of eighteen.

Erikson's theory of ego development saw the adolescent mind as a 'mind of the moratorium' and youth as a period of 'structured irresponsibility' (Jones, 2009). However, Jahoda and Warren (1965, cited in Jones, 2009) argued that in traditional societies, where physiological maturity and social maturity occur simultaneously, there are no problems with youth. It is only in industrialised societies, where there is neither appropriate training for adulthood nor a sure place in the social world, that young people face an adjustment problem and could find themselves temporarily in a 'marginal world' (Reuter, 1937, cited in Jones, 2009). This prolonged emotional, psychological, and economic dependency led to a century-long enduring mythology of adolescence, depicted as a period of 'storm and stress' subject to hormonally induced mood swings (Ruddick, 2003). Thus 'adolescent disorder' is not biological, but socially constructed.

As childhood is now seen as a period when the real world of sexual, economic, and public action is suspended, children who assume a different position within the generational hierarchy are considered a social and moral threat (Wyness, 2012). In fact, without opportunities for productive civic engagement, young people's frustrations can boil over into violent behaviour and lead to economic and social instability, sparks that can ignite long-simmering disputes (World Bank, 2006). 'Juvenile delinquency', especially with reference to status offences, is thus socially constructed. Status offenders are children who commit an act that violates a law or ordinance designed to regulate behaviour with reference to age. Status offences, therefore, need to be decriminalised.

2.4 Implications of Industrialisation and Globalisation for Childhood

On one hand, the social construction of childhood and adolescence has made all children vulnerable. On the other hand, industrialisation and globalisation have brought about far-reaching changes in economic, societal, as well as family structures, that have led to several positive changes, but also aggravated problems in childhood. With industrialisation, societies have become more modern, family has become nuclear, community orientation has loosened, and kinship supports for families have weakened. This nuclear family type is characterised by aggravation of patriarchy by housewifisation of women and increases in family violence, dual career families, consumerism, and individualism, etc.

Globalisation is the development of an increasingly integrated world-wide economy marked by free trade, free flow of capital, and the tapping of cheaper foreign labour markets that transcend nation-state boundaries. An increasingly integrated world economy enables human trafficking to thrive. Comparative advantage in goods and cheap labour in developing states have played significant roles in objectifying and exploiting humans for economic ends. Women and children are the most vulnerable and thus, principal victims of traffickers who coerce their services, predominantly in the sex industries (Brewer, 2008).

Globalisation has made the poor poorer and more vulnerable due to weakened social structures that ordinarily serve as a safety net to help meet basic needs. As more families drift towards the social and economic margins of society, their children's vulnerability to commercial exploitation is exacerbated (ECPAT, 2014). Households that had expected to receive state assistance find themselves made vulnerable as the state–citizen relationship has been redefined. Middle-class citizens who had previously received services were told that they were no longer entitled to these benefits or entitled only if they could afford to pay for those provided on a cost-recovery basis. The lower income groups, many of whom had never received such benefits, continue to be ignored (Mitlin & Hickey, 2009).

2.5 Universal Comprehensive and Longitudinal Conceptual Framework of Problems in Childhood

A conceptual framework that is universal, comprehensive, and longitudinal is proposed here to deconstruct problems in childhood. This framework addresses the problems of overlaps of terms used with specificities, includes problems faced worldwide instead of focusing only on those that are faced by children in the Western countries, and identifies linkages among problems in childhood in the context of family and community. As a universal approach is needed, the definitions, causes, and effects for those problems are identified mainly from the international literature developed by the UN bodies and by international non-government organisations.

2.5.1 Vulnerability in Childhood

The social construction of childhood helps to identify the common causal factors of problems in childhood. All children are made vulnerable due to adultism that leads to protective exclusion, dependence, and absence of agency. Sexism has further marginalised girls, ableism has marginalised children with disability, and racism and casteism have marginalised children of marginalised races/castes/indigenous people/tribes. These prejudicing ideologies lead to discrimination, exclusion, and marginalisation.

2.5.2 Poverty in Childhood

According to the UN Report on the World's Social Situation (UN, 2010) on the theme of rethinking poverty, the concept of social exclusion contributes to an understanding of the nature of poverty and helps to identify the causes of poverty that may have been otherwise neglected. Social exclusion exists across all societies in numerous and often compounded forms, affecting people of all ages and backgrounds. Industrialisation has led to poverty among marginalised communities, migrant and nomadic families, unemployed/unorganised labour, landless and marginal farmers, and urban slum dwellers. Discrimination and social exclusion increase the socio-economic stresses on families and make it more likely that their children migrate to the streets (Consortium for Street Children & Plan, 2011). Technology has led to increased migration together with increased unemployment among men whose labour is replaced by automatic machines. Such unemployment has resulted in a major expansion of the unprotected, unorganised labour force. This force includes an increasing number of women, who were left out of development projects, and children. The unorganised sector does not provide social security and scope for unionisation or application of anti-discrimination laws and so on. The increased magnitude of the unorganised sector has led to increased poverty among female-headed families or feminisation of poverty. Such circumstances put families under severe strain as increasing instability erodes their capacity to act as the frontline of protection for their children (ECPAT, 2014).

Besides families of marginalised communities, families in poverty include families of landless and marginal farmers, migrant and nomadic families, families of unemployed/unorganised labour, families living in slums/on the footpath/ street, etc. Poverty is the main factor that makes children vulnerable to commercial exploitation. Girls from poor families are vulnerable to commercial exploitation through labour in the unorganised sector, sale, trafficking, and prostitution, leading to increase in teenage pregnancy, and HIV/AIDS. Boys from poor families seem to be relatively more vulnerable than girls to labour in the organised sector, physical abuse, substance abuse, and conflict with law (Desai, 2018).

According to the UN General Assembly (2007):

> Children living in poverty are deprived of nutrition, water and sanitation facilities, access to basic health-care services, shelter, education, participation and protection, and that while a severe lack of goods and services hurts every human being, it is most threatening and harmful to children, leaving them unable to enjoy their rights, to reach their full potential and to participate as full members of the society.

The UN General Assembly recognised the special nature of poverty for children, stating clearly that child poverty is about more than just a lack of money, and can only be understood as the denial of a range of rights laid out in the UN Convention on the Rights of the Child. The Christian Children's Fund (CCF, 2005) views child poverty as comprising three inter-related domains: Deprivation is a lack of material conditions and services generally held to be essential to the development of children's full potential; exclusion is the result of unjust processes through which children's dignity, voice, and rights are denied, or their existence threatened; and vulnerability is an inability of society to cope with existing or probable threats to children in their environment.

2.5.3 Neglect of Meeting Basic Needs of Children

Neglect is frequently defined as the failure of a parent or other person with responsibility for the child to provide the child with food, clothing, shelter, medical care, or supervision to the degree that the child's health, safety, and well-being are threatened with harm (Child Welfare Information Gateway, 2014). Because parents are the main caregivers of children, at the micro level the cause of child neglect is inadequate parental care. However, several individual and systemic factors are at play for such parental inadequacy. The Global Survey on Violence against Children, conducted under the auspices of the Special Representative of the Secretary General (SRSG) on Violence against Children (2013), confirmed that the most vulnerable children are those with disabilities, those who migrate, those who are confined to institutions, and those whose poverty and social exclusion expose them to deprivation, neglect, and at times to the inherent dangers of life on the streets. Children at risk of neglect are grouped into marginalised children, invisible children, children of families living in poverty, children of single-parent families, and children in families with other difficult situations.

Marginalised or excluded children at risk of neglect are girls, children with disabilities, and children of marginalised communities, due to prejudicing ideologies such as sexism, ableism, racism, casteism, etc. School dropouts and children in institutions are invisible children, as they are neither covered by school programmes, nor by the programmes of civil society organisations. Social exclusion has been defined by the Department of International Development (DFID, 2005, p. 3) as 'a process by which certain groups are systematically disadvantaged because they are discriminated against on the basis of their ethnicity, race, religion, sexual orientation, caste, descent, gender, age, disability, HIV status, migrant status or where they live'.

Children of single-parent families in poverty groups would include children of unwed parents or sex workers, children of incarcerated parents, and children whose one parent has migrated, deserted, or died, or whose parents have separated or divorced, are in poverty groups, etc. Children from single-parent families, although still in parental care, are at risk as the remaining parent struggles to support the family as well as care for the children. This risk is particularly prevalent among children of female-headed households which may be excluded from economic opportunities (ECPAT, 2006). Children are at risk of neglect also when their families are affected by substance use, HIV, terminal illness, domestic violence, etc.

Children in at-risk situations are vulnerable to neglect of adequate food, clothing, shelter, medical care, or supervision to the degree that the child's health, development, safety, and well-being are affected. Moreover, these children are vulnerable to taking on adult responsibilities, separation from parents, abuse, commercial exploitation, and conflict with law.

2.5.4 Parent–Child Separation

According to the UN Guidelines for the Alternative Care of Children (2010), children without parental care are:

> [A]ll children not in the overnight care of at least one of their parents, for whatever reason and under whatever circumstances. Children without parental care may be designated as:
>
> i. "Unaccompanied" if they are not cared for by another relative or an adult who by law or custom is responsible for doing so; or
> ii. "Separated" if they are separated from a previous legal or customary primary caregiver, but who may nevertheless be accompanied by another relative.'

Children without parental care can also be classified into (1) children who have living parents but are away from them and (2) children who do not have living parents, also called orphans. According to the Interagency Guiding Principles on Unaccompanied and Separated Children (International Committee of the Red Cross, 2004), orphans are children both of whose parents are known to be dead. The usage of the term 'orphan' for a child who has lost one parent is confusing, so needs to be avoided.

Children without parental care may be living on the street, in institutions or as child-headed households. In many emergencies or crisis situations, groups of children are left without any adult to care for them. In these households, an older child or young adult may assume responsibility as head of the household. Such child-headed households often – although not exclusively – occur in sibling groups (Save the Children, 2004).

Parent–child separation can occur in any of the following three ways: voluntary separation, accidental separation, or abduction/trafficking. Voluntary separation may take place when parents who feel unable to care for children, or believe their children will be safer or have more opportunities elsewhere, entrust children to a neighbour or stranger for safekeeping or take them to an orphanage or abandon them; or children leave their families intentionally due to lack of food and resources, or abuse. Accidental separations generally occur when conflict or natural disasters force individuals, families, and communities to flee without warning, or during large-scale organised population movements. Children may have been away from home when their families had to flee during an armed attack or may have been left unattended when parents were away from home. Children can also become separated during the chaos of flight, either at the onset or during travel as some members of the family stop to rest or wander from the group (Save the Children, 2004). Children may be abducted/trafficked for ransom, sale, forced labour, or recruitment in armed conflict.

Children without parental care are vulnerable to inadequate food, clothing, shelter, medical care, or supervision to the degree that the child's health, development, safety, and well-being are affected. These children are vulnerable to taking on adult responsibilities, abuse, commercial exploitation, and conflict with law. Moreover, children without parental care are deprived of the closest emotional bond in their lives.

2.5.5 Violence against Children

The international discourse in the field of child protection has moved towards a more 'violence-based' language (ECPAT International, 2016). Over their lifetime, children exposed to violence are at increased risk of mental illness and anxiety disorders; high-risk behaviours like alcohol and drug abuse, smoking and unsafe sex; chronic diseases such as cancers, diabetes, and heart disease; infectious diseases like HIV; and social problems including educational under-attainment, further involvement in violence, and crime (WHO, 2020).

Violence includes child abuse as well as commercial exploitation of children, and it is necessary to differentiate between these two forms of violence against children. Child abuse is any intentional non-accidental physical, emotional, and psychological and/or sexual harm done to a child, that endangers or impairs the child's physical, emotional, and psychological or sexual health and development. This harm can be carried out by older/stronger children, spouse/partner, parents, relatives, caregivers, neighbours, teachers, employers, police, or strangers; in family, neighbourhood, street, school, institutions, workplace, or police/judicial custody (adapted from Desai, 2010). It includes corporal punishment and bullying.

As far as commercial exploitation of children is concerned, its definition can be based on the definition of commercial sexual exploitation of children (CSEC), by the Stockholm Declaration and Agenda for Action (1996): 'It comprises sexual abuse by the adult and remuneration in cash or kind to the child or a third person or persons. The child is treated as a sexual object and as a commercial object' (cited by ECPAT International, 2016). Thus, in commercial exploitation of children, child abuse is connected with cash or in-kind profit for the child and/or adult third person or persons. The third person or persons who make a profit out of this abuse, that is, the procurers or agents, are part of the commercial and/or criminal nexus, comprising largely men, but also women. Commercial exploitation of children comprises exploitation of children for labour, CSEC, and trafficking and sale of children (Desai, 2019).

2.5.6 Child Abuse

Violence through child abuse is in-built into patriarchal families as power leads to abuse of the less powerful. With the nuclearisation of family, the separation of private and public spheres, the increased commodification of relationships and weak community supports, vulnerability of the less powerful members in families to domestic violence has increased. Everything that happens within the four walls of the nuclear family is considered a private matter and no outside intervention is encouraged. Family violence, therefore, often remains invisible, undiscussed, and unchallenged (Bhasin, 2000). Feminist theorisation identifies male power, hegemony, and socialisation as the key causal factors not only for violence against women, but for child abuse also (Corby, 2002). Critical theorists opine that child abuse is systemic or structural (Burman, 2008) based in adultism, patriarchy, and vulnerability of marginalised children. As a result, violence against children is both common and widespread – and no society is without some level of violence against its youngest members.

Although children are vulnerable to neglect and abuse in traditional patriarchal families, these children do grow up among family and community support. However, nuclearisation of the family has aggravated adultism and may reduce parental capacity to care for children, making them more vulnerable to neglect and abuse. At the family level, it can also be an outcome of problems with family dynamics and individual psychosocial or psychiatric problems of the abuser.

The World Report on Violence against Children by the independent expert for the UN, Pinheiro (2006), identified violence against children in the home and family, schools and educational settings, care and justice institutions, places of work, and the community. According to him, physical and psychological violence, sexual abuse, and sexual harassment are forms of violence which occur in all settings.

The neglected children and those separated from parents, are especially vulnerable to child abuse. Pinheiro (2006) noted that children with disabilities, orphaned children (including those orphaned by AIDS), indigenous children, children from ethnic minorities and other marginalised groups, children living or working on the streets, children in institutions and detention, children living in communities in which inequality, unemployment, and poverty are highly concentrated, and child refugees and other displaced children, are vulnerable to violence. Of course, abuse takes place across classes, but the upper classes may be able to conceal it because of access to greater resources and less scrutiny by social services (Downs, Moore, & McFadden, 2009). Data confirm that some types of child abuse, such as violent discipline, affect children from rich and poor households alike (UNICEF, 2017). Pinheiro (2006) noted that young children are at greatest risk of physical abuse whereas adolescents are at greater risk of sexual abuse; and boys are more at risk of physical abuse than girls and girls are at greater risk of sexual abuse.

ECPAT International, Plan International, Save the Children, UNICEF, and World Vision carried out a review and analysis of mappings and assessments of National Child Protection Systems in the East Asia and Pacific Region in 2014. They found that measured against broader international thresholds that define notions of physical violence, there are higher levels of tolerance in the countries studied. In countries where community harmony rather than individual rights is of primary importance, harsh physical punishment is considered as good, attentive parenting. By disciplining a child harshly, a parent is educating the child about common community values and provides greater opportunity for that child to thrive among peers. This pattern of disciplining the child is seen predominantly in the less-developed countries of the region but holds true also in middle-income countries. The threshold of discipline-abuse in many countries is only crossed if a child is made to bleed or bones are broken.

Child or early marriage is often used as a commercial exploitation of children, especially girls (for example, Inter-Parliamentary Union & UNICEF, 2005). However, it may be more appropriate to include it under child abuse as it is definitely abusive but may or may not have a commercial angle. The UN report of 2014 defined 'child marriage' as a marriage in which at least one of the parties is a child, a person aged below eighteen. 'Early marriage' is often used interchangeably with 'child marriage' and refers to marriages involving a person aged below eighteen.

Although practices such as female circumcision and child marriages are considered abusive in the Western culture, children who are subjected to them, however painful and terrifying, often view them as having a positive long-term value. It is important to note that the child's view of his or her experience and treatment has long been recognised as an important consideration in differentiating cultural practices from abuse (Korbin, 2003). Koramoa, Lynch, and Kinnair (2002) stress the need to provide some middle ground between absolutist and culturally relative concepts of abuse. They distinguish between traditional cultural practices that enhance a child's cultural identity and those that cause harm.

Beyond the unnecessary hurt and pain it causes, violence undermines children's sense of self-worth and hinders their development. Yet, it may be tacitly accepted due to the familiarity of perpetrators or minimised as inconsequential. The memory or reporting of violence may be buried due to shame or fear of reprisal. Impunity of perpetrators and prolonged exposure may leave victims believing violence is normal. In such ways, violence is masked, making it difficult to prevent and end (UNICEF, 2017). Abuse in childhood undermines children's sense of self-worth, with emotions of shame and fear, makes them submissive and tolerant, and hinders their development and relationships.

2.5.7 Commercial Exploitation of Children

As discussed earlier, in commercial exploitation of children, child abuse is connected with cash or in-kind profit for the child and/or adult third person or persons. The third person or persons who make a profit out of this abuse, that is, the procurers or agents, are part of the commercial and/or criminal nexus, comprising largely men, but also women. Commercial exploitation of children comprises exploitation of children for labour, child and early marriages, CSEC, and trafficking and sale of children (Desai, 2019).

Children worked at home in the preindustrial era and in factories after industrialisation. However, with the advent of schooling and recognition of the importance of education, child labour was identified as a problem. According to the ILO (n.d.):

> The term 'child labour' is often defined as work that deprives children of their childhood, their potential and their dignity, and that is harmful to physical and mental development. It refers to work that:
>
> i. is mentally, physically, socially, or morally dangerous and harmful to children; and/or
> ii. interferes with their schooling by depriving them of the opportunity to attend school; obliging them to leave school prematurely; or requiring them to attempt to combine school attendance with excessively long and heavy work.

Children's or adolescents' participation in work that does not affect their health and personal development or interfere with their schooling, is generally regarded as being something positive. This includes activities such as helping their parents around the home, assisting in a family business, or earning pocket money outside school hours and during school holidays. These kinds of activities contribute to children's development and to the welfare of their families; provide children with skills and experience; and help to prepare them to be productive members of society during their adult life (ILO, n.d.).

CSEC through child prostitution, child sex tourism, and child pornography, are relatively recently identified as problems. According to the ILO (2008),

'Commercial sexual exploitation of children is the sexual exploitation by an adult of a child or adolescent below eighteen years of age that involves a transaction in cash or in kind to the child or to one or more third parties. It is an abhorrent violation of the human rights of children and is without question one of the worst forms of child labour.' It further states that, 'Commercial sexual exploitation of children includes the use of girls and boys in sexual activities remunerated in cash or in kind; trafficking of girls and boys and adolescents for the sex trade; child sex tourism; the production, promotion and distribution of pornography involving children; and, the use of children in sex shows (public or private)' (ILO, 2008).

Such commercial exploitation of children is facilitated by child trafficking and sale. According to the UN Protocol to Prevent, Suppress and Punish Trafficking in Persons Especially Women and Children (2000), supplementing the UN Convention against Transnational Organized Crime, 'trafficking in persons' shall mean:

> the recruitment, transportation, transfer, harbouring or receipt of persons, by means of the threat or use of force or other forms of coercion, of abduction, of fraud, of deception, of the abuse of power or of a position of vulnerability or of the giving or receiving of payments or benefits to achieve the consent of a person having control over another person, for the purpose of exploitation. Exploitation shall include, at a minimum, the exploitation of the prostitution of others or other forms of sexual exploit- ation, forced labour or services, slavery, or practices similar to slavery, servitude, or the removal of organs.

The first Special Rapporteur on the sale of children, child prostitution, and child pornography identified, in a report in 1993, the following forms of sale of children: sale by adoption, sale for child labour exploitation, and sale of children's organs (ECPAT International, 2016).

The literature talks about causes of child labour, child and early marriages, CSEC, and trafficking and sale of children separately. Clubbing them together under commercial exploitation of children has advantages as their causes of supply and demand are similar. Poverty is the apparent cause for supply of children for all kinds of commercial exploitation. Some poor parents sell their children, not just for the money, but also in the hope that their children will escape a situation of chronic poverty and move to a place where they will have a better life and more opportunities (UNODC, 2008). The Inter-Agency Coordination Group against Trafficking in Persons (2018) notes that children living in poverty, who are out of school, are more likely to be working under exploitative conditions and less likely to have access to safety nets, which can make them more vulner- able to trafficking. Besides family, school is another system that protects children from commercial exploitation. Children separated from parents and/or out of school children are particularly vulnerable to commercial exploitation. Migrants, refugees, and internally displaced children are also at risk of being trafficking. Children are more vulnerable to trafficking when these factors are coupled with inadequate education, healthcare, and social protection systems, as well as statelessness, poverty, discrimination, and organised crime. War and civil strife may lead to massive displacements of populations, leaving orphans and street children extremely vulnerable to trafficking (UNODC, 2008).

Children from poverty groups are commodified as there is an increasing demand for them. Consumerism has increased demands for cheap labour and free sex that make children's exploitation a profitable business. As socioeconomically disadvantaged people improvise to salvage a livelihood in a transforming world, opportunistic predators seize upon the vulnerability of the desperate (Brewer, 2008). Truong (2001) noted that organised crime finds its market niche in various forms of transnational population movements spurred by forces of globalisation which render the livelihood of particular segments of the world population insecure in a political as well as economic sense. Moreover, there is an ongoing intrusion of market values into regulating the treatment of the human body as a commodity. Thus, beyond and above the issue of human rights abuse, there is a need to set the terms of the discussion on human trafficking as an aspect of international trade by organised crime.

Child victims of commercial sexual exploitation suffer severe physical and psychological harm. They not only risk injuries from physical violence, unwanted pregnancies, and HIV/AIDS and other sexually transmitted diseases, they also lose self-esteem, feel humiliation, guilt, and sadness, and may develop problems with verbal and written communication. Once entrapped in the sex trade, it is difficult for them to break loose. They may live in fear of retribution and have to bear the additional traumas of social stigmatisation, marginalisation, and even rejection by their families and . At this point, their prospects for decent work as adults are limited (ILO, n.d.).

2.5.8 Conflict with Law in Childhood

The UNODC (2013) defined a 'child in conflict with the law' as a child alleged as, accused of, or recognised as having infringed the criminal law. 'Children in conflict with law' describes the situation the child is in, as against 'juvenile delinquent' which labels the child. Conflict with law in childhood includes status offences, property offences, and violent offences (Desai, 2010, p. 382). Status offenders are children who commit an act that violates a law or ordinance designed to regulate his or her behaviour because of his or her age or status.

Status offences are solely based on the offender's age and are unique to juveniles (I prefer to call them children). Anyone above the legal age who engages in the same behaviours would not be committing an offence (Hess & Drowns, 2004). Examples of status offences are smoking and drinking, not going to school, coming home late, etc.

Save the Children (2005) stated that the overwhelming majority of children in conflict with the law (over 90 per cent) are petty offenders, who mainly commit offences against property and four out of five children who commit an offence only commit one in their lifetime. Murder, sexual offences, school bullying, and juvenile gangs are manifestations of violent offences. The violent offenders also include children associated with armed forces or armed groups.

Labelling children as 'juvenile delinquents' itself makes children develop an identity of and behave as delinquents. As discussed earlier, the scientific construction of 'normal' childhood and adolescence, leading to the formulation of status offences, make the so-called 'deviants' delinquents. Save the Children (2004) noted that poverty, neglect, and abuse are the major causes of children getting in conflict with law. Large numbers of children in conflict with law are socio-economic victims, many of whom have had little or no access to education; many are working children. Some children leave their homes and take to the streets to escape from violence and abuse at the hands of their families. Some are forced to make a living on the streets, in order to survive. Others are abandoned by their families and left to fend for themselves and sometimes for younger siblings. These children are at high risk of becoming involved in substance abuse and the drug trade through peer influence or the influence of adult criminals. They are driven towards coping strategies that will in turn expose them to further violence and the increasing risk of coming into conflict with the law.

Another factor responsible for children's conflict with law is learning disabilities such as dyslexia and attention deficit disorder. They do not cause delinquency, but in the absence of understanding by the society, these disabilities place children/youth at greater risk of conflict with law. School failure, poorly developed social skills, and inadequate school and community supports are associated with the over-representation of youth with disabilities at all stages of the juvenile justice system (The National Center on Education, Disability and Juvenile Justice, n.d.).

As the National Commission for Protection of Child Rights (2010) noted, there is a fundamental lack of understanding and recognition within the juvenile justice system that children in conflict with law are also children in need of care and protection; children in need of care and protection are also at risk of becoming children in conflict with law; and all 'at-risk' children are also potential entitlement holders within the juvenile justice system.

Children get further criminalised by the approach of the justice system for children, which has generally been retributive. Lack of confidentiality and insensitive treatment by law enforcement agencies and the courts aggravate children's problems. More serious than the inaction by the state are acts of commission against children, such as their arrest, detention, and torture (UNICEF, 2004). Beyond their exposure to violence, children who are detained are further removed from any support mechanisms that they may have had and further isolated from the socialising influence of their communities. Instead, they are de-socialised and learn to survive only by the rules of coercion and power that are evident in the prison environment. Any socialisation that does take place is often at the hands of other more experienced inmates, which only serves to ensure the further criminalisation of the child (Save the Children, 2004).

2.5.9 Children in Emergencies

The Child Protection Working Group (CPWG, 2012, p. 13) defined a crisis or emergency as a threatening condition that requires urgent action. It leads to widespread human, material, economic or environmental losses and impacts that exceed the ability of the affected community or society to cope using its own resources, and which therefore requires urgent action. The CPWG states that emergencies can result from natural hazards, or are human-made, or a combination of both. These include natural disasters, pandemics, armed conflict, internal displacement, statelessness, refugee situation, etc. The effects of an emergency on a community depend on the type and extent of the emergency, the level of organisation and stability of the state before and during the emergency, and the community's capacity to respond (CPWG, 2012). The Inter-Agency Standing Committee (IASC, 2011) noted that pre-existing vulner-abilities and patterns of discrimination usually become exacerbated in situations of natural disasters.

According to the Interagency Modular Training Package (2008), during emergency situations, children suffer because of several reasons. Facilities such as schools and health centres are damaged or destroyed and do not function. The basic needs of children may not be met, and their development can be hindered. Children also suffer from psychological disturbances, and feelings of fears, anxiety, mistrust, and sadness that have long-lasting effects. Children may suffer the loss of access to adequate food, healthcare, education, and basic social services. Moreover, children may be continually exposed to danger, which may result in loss of life and limb, abuse, exploitation, and neglect. In this chaotic situation, children are at risk of neglect, parent–child separation, abuse, commercial exploitation, and conflict with law.

2.5.10 Children in Armed Conflicts

In the late 20th and the early 21st centuries, the term 'armed conflict' replaced that of 'war'. There is no universally accepted definition of the term; however, the Office for the Coordination of Humanitarian Affairs defines armed conflict as: 'A dispute involving the use of armed force between two or more parties' (International Bureau for Children's Rights, 2010). The International Bureau for Children's Rights (2010) notes that the term 'armed conflict' covers a much broader spectrum of violence than does 'war' and is marked by a high level of fluidity and fragmentation. The Paris Principles and Guidelines on Children associated with Armed Forces or Armed Groups (CAAFAG) (2007) define the following:

i. Armed Forces refer to the military institution of a State with a legal basis, and supporting institutional infrastructure (salaries, benefits, basic services, etc.).
ii. Armed Groups refer to groups distinct from armed forces as defined by Article 4 of the Optional Protocol to the Convention on the Rights of the Child on the involvement of children in armed conflict.

In recent decades, children have been increasingly affected and targeted by armed conflicts. In 2005, the UN Security Council identified six categories of grave violations against children in armed conflict as serious breaches and violations of applicable international law: recruitment or use of children as soldiers, killing or maiming of children, sexual violence against children, attacks against schools or hospitals, abduction of children, and denial of humanitarian access for children (UNICEF, 2009).

According to the Paris Principles (2007), a CAAFAG refers to any person below eighteen years of age who is or who has been recruited or used by an armed force or armed group in any capacity, including but not limited to children, boys and girls, used as fighters, cooks, porters, messengers, spies, or for sexual purposes. It does not only refer to a child who is taking or has taken a direct part in hostilities. The CAAFAGs are exposed to tremendous violence – often forced both to witness and commit violence, while themselves being abused, forced to use drugs, exploited, injured, or even killed as a result. Their condition deprives them of their rights, often with severe physical and emotional long-term consequences, including disabilities, as a result of their experiences (CPWG, 2012).

According to the Interagency Modular Training Package (2008), child recruitment into armed forces or groups can be compulsory or forced by the armed group or armed force, or children may voluntarily join them for several reasons. According to the Interagency Modular Training Package,

reasons for armed forces and groups recruiting children are easy manipula-
tion, absence of laws, lack of documents, and proliferation of small arms. It
noted that while all types of children are recruited, the following children
are more at risk of recruitment by armed forces or armed groups: adolescents; children separated from their families (unaccompanied children,
separated children, orphans, abandoned children, street children, children
living in institutions); marginalised children, including those from particular ethnic, racial or religious groups; refugee and displaced children; children who are economically and/or socially disadvantaged; children who are
mistreated or exploited in their families; children living in conflict zones or
occupied territories; children living in highly militarised communities;
children living in areas where the government is not able to adequately
protect them; and children formerly associated with armed forces or groups,

There is usually a combination of 'push and pull factors' behind a child's
decision to join an armed force or armed group voluntarily. It means that a child
who joins voluntarily may have done so because he or she had little alternative
(Interagency Modular Training Package, 2008). According to the Interagency
Modular Training Package (2008), reasons for children voluntarily joining armed
conflict include poverty, lack of access to education or training, social or cultural
discrimination, glorification of military life, revenge, security provided by armed
forces/groups, and belief in the ideology of the armed forces/groups:

2.5.11 Effects in Childhood and Implications for Adult Life

Neglect, separation from parents, abuse, and commercial exploitation in childhood result in further vulnerability to neglect, abuse, and commercial exploitation as children lose self-respect and dignity, leading to submissiveness and
tolerance to more abuse and exploitation. When not addressed, problems in
childhood continue as a cycle when relapse of abuse and exploitation take place,
abuse leads to exploitation or from one type of exploitation to another or to
conflict with the law, or first-time delinquents becoming chronic delinquents.
Children's basic needs of education, recreation, and cultural life are disrupted,
and they develop lifelong problems with physical, mental, and emotional health
and development, and social relationships, as well as career.

Children's well-being is crucial not only for their well-being in childhood,
but for their well-being as adults and that of their children as well. It is,
therefore, vulnerability in childhood as a stage of human life that we are
concerned with, for the well-being in subsequent life stages and subsequent
generations. The implications of neglect, abuse, commercial exploitation, conflict with law or association with armed conflict in childhood are

submissiveness and tolerance to more abuse and exploitation. These character-istics continue in their adult life. The prejudicing ideologies of adultism, sexism, etc. are recycled as the survivor becomes an abuser/exploiter as an adult and abuses and exploits their own or others' children and other vulnerable groups.

2.6 Summary

This Element's section on Problems in Childhood starts with identification of problems with the concepts used for problems in childhood. The first problem is that the terms neglect, abuse, maltreatment, violence, and exploitation are often used synonymously. The terms do overlap as abuse always amounts to violence and maltreatment and both are often exploitative. However, the terms need to be distinguished and made specific. The second problem is dominance of the Western conceptualisation of problems in childhood that needs to be replaced with a universal framework. The third problem identified is the need to under-stand the linkages among problems in childhood in the context of family and community, in order to understand the cycle of problems as well as the differ-ential context, manifestations, and consequences in each problem situation.

The Element then discusses how all children are made vulnerable due to adultism that leads to protective exclusion, and sexism has further marginalised girls as children as well as females. The social construction of childhood through schooling has led to dependence of children on adults and weakened the agency of children. Social construction of 'normal' childhood by Western development sciences has led to universal chronologisation, based on Western, white, middle-class, male constructs of 'normality'. It comprises children and adolescents as innocent, asexual, financially illiterate, and apolitical; and any 'deviance' is considered a disorder. With extension of education, childhood is constructed up to the age of eighteen, including adolescence in childhood. Now chronologisation has created an artificial dichotomy between childhood and adulthood, as though the two are distinctly different from one another. Moreover, the prolonged emotional, psychological, and economic dependency has led to depiction of adolescence as a period of 'storm and stress'.

Finally, the Element proposes a universal comprehensive and longitudinal conceptual framework of problems in childhood, their differential context, and their cyclical effects. Based on the linkages identified in children's problems, they are divided into three consecutive levels: primary, secondary, and tertiary. The primary level problems are problems due to social exclusion that lead to second-ary and tertiary levels of problems if not addressed. The secondary level of problems are problems due to poverty and neglect, that lead to tertiary level of problems if not addressed. The tertiary level problems are sociolegal problems that require the justice system. This framework is important for planning preventive services at primary, secondary, and tertiary levels to break the cycle of problems in childhood and their implications for adult life.

For details, see Table 1.

3 Conceptual Framework of Service Delivery Systems for Child Welfare

3.1 Overview

This Element's section on Conceptual Framework of Service Delivery Systems for Child Welfare starts with discussion of the concepts of service delivery of child welfare, child protection, and juvenile justice. It then reviews the service delivery approaches in this field with reference to their limitations, because of which these services have not helped to break the cycle of problems in childhood. The Element identifies the rights-based, comprehensive, preventive, and systemic conceptual framework of service delivery systems for child welfare through Family Service Centres. This framework helps to develop service delivery for children at primary, secondary, and tertiary prevention levels, to meet the needs of all children, poor and neglected children, and children facing sociolegal problems, respectively, in order to break the cycle of problems at these levels.

3.2 Concepts and Review of Service Delivery of Child Welfare, Child Protection, and Juvenile Justice

3.2.1 Concepts and Review of Child Welfare Services

Child welfare means the well-being of children and child welfare services are services that promote the well-being of children. Because the family is regarded as the primary child welfare system and parents are the primary caregivers, when family or parents have problems, their role of providing for the well-being of the child is affected. The state or voluntary organisations need to support, supplement, or substitute parental childcare in these situations. Kadushin and Martin (1988) had, therefore, classified child welfare services into supplemental, supportive, and substitutive. Supplementary child welfare services include day/night care/drop-in centres, and before/after school care. Supportive child welfare services include counselling for child and parents/caregivers, services for financial support, legal aid, and linkages to supplementary and substitute child welfare services. Substitute child welfare is also known as alternative childcare. These services include foster family care, adoption, and institutional childcare.

Table 1 Universal comprehensive and longitudinal conceptual framework of problems in childhood

Problems in childhood	Causes of problems	Vulnerable children	Effects of problems on children
Primary Level Problems: Problems Due to Social Exclusion			
Vulnerability in Childhood ↔	adultism	sll children	• protective exclusion • dependence • absence of agency • children considered innocent, asexual, financially illiterate, & apolitical • 'deviance' from the western norms considered a disorder
	sexism, ableism, racism, & casteism	• girls • children with disability • children of marginalised races/castes/indigenous people/tribes	• discrimination • social exclusion • marginalisation
Secondary Level Problems: Problems due to Poverty and Neglect			
Poverty in childhood ↔	• marginalisation/exclusion of races/castes/indigenous peoples/tribes • industrialisation • globalisation	Children of: • marginalised communities • migrant & nomadic families • unemployed/unorganised labour	• neglect of meeting basic needs • living on the street • child labour • vulnerable to commercial sexual exploitation

Table 1 (cont.)

Problems in childhood	Causes of problems	Vulnerable children	Effects of problems on children
Neglect of meeting basic needs ↩	• unemployment • feminisation of poverty • inadequate parental care due to poverty • marginalisation & social exclusion • single-parenthood	• landless & marginal farmers • urban slum & pavement dwellers • female-headed families • marginalised children • children in poverty • children of single-parent families • children on the street • children of families affected by substance use/other problems	• neglect of meeting basic needs • vulnerable to separation from parents, violence, & conflict with law
Tertiary Level Problems: Sociolegal Problems			
Parent-child separation: • children living on the street • child-headed households • children in institutions ↩	• voluntary separation due to poverty/abuse • accidental separation during emergencies • trafficking/sale • death of both parents	• children who have living parents but are away from them • children who do not have living parents/orphans	• neglect of meeting basic needs • taking on adult responsibilities • vulnerable to abuse, commercial exploitation, & conflict with law

	Causes	Affected children	Consequences
Child abuse: • Physical abuse/ corporal punishment • Sexual buse • Psychological/ emotional abuse • Child marriage ↑	• adultism, sexism, ableism, racism, & casteism • nuclearisation of family • increased commodification of relationships • weak community supports • culture-based practices	• marginsalised children • neglected children • children without parental care • children in institutions • commercially exploitated children	• harms children's sense of self-worth • creates emotions of guilt, shame, & fear • makes them submissive & tolerant to violence • hinders their development & relationships
Commercial exploitation of children: • Child labour • Commercial sexual exploitation • Trafficking & sale ↑	• poverty • lack of school enrolment • neglect of meeting basic needs • demands for cheap labour & free sex • international organised crime	• marginalised children • neglected children • children without parental care • children in poverty • child refugees, stateless children, & internally displaced children	• severe physical & psychological harm • harms children's sense of self-worth • creates emotions of guilt, shame, & fear • risk unwanted pregnancies, hiv/aids, & other sexually transmitted diseases • face social stigma, marginalisation, & rejection by their families & communities
Conflict with law in childhood: • status offences	• poverty • neglect of meeting basic needs	• out of school children • children on street • substance using children	retributive justice approach leads to: • violence • detention

Table 1 (cont.)

Problems in childhood	Causes of problems	Vulnerable children	Effects of problems on children
• petty crimes • violent Crimes ↔	• commercial exploitation of children • deviation from 'normal' behaviour • learning disabilities	• child refugees • stateless children • internally displaced children	• isolation from family & community • recriminalisation
Effects in Childhood ↔	• long-term physical, mental, emotional and social effects on children and their family life & career • submissiveness & tolerance to more abuse & exploitation in childhood & adult life		
Implications for Adult Life ↔	• adultism, sexism, ableism, racism, & casteism are recycled • survivors become abusers/exploiters of their own or others' children & other vulnerable groups		

Table 2 Conceptual framework for rights-based comprehensive, preventive, and systemic child welfare

Target Groups	Goals	Systems	Services
Primary Level Prevention Services			
All Children	1. Prevent children's vulnerability based in adultism, sexism, ableism, racism, & casteism 2. Promote children's development and empowerment	• Schools	• Integrated Child Development & Empowerment Services
Secondary Level Prevention Services			
Poor & Neglected Children	1. Address their marginalisation, invisibility, poverty, and other difficult situations 2. Prevent exclusion, neglect, violence, parental separation, & conflict with law	• Community-based Family Service Centres	• Poverty Eradication for Families • Financial Assistance/ Sponsorship for Children • Integrated Supplementary Childcare Services • Integrated Family & Child Support Services • Integrated Child Development & Empowerment Services

Table 2 (cont.)

Target Groups	Goals	Systems	Services
Tertiary Level Prevention Services			
Children with Sociolegal Problems:	1. Provide sociolegal justice to these children and rehabilitate them 2. Prevent secondary victimisation & relapse of the same or other problems	• District-based Extended Family Service Centres with Departments:	
• Children Deprived of Parental Care		Department of Integrated Alternative Childcare	• Family Strengthening and Prevention of Child-Family Separation • Legal Placement in Foster Family Care, Adoption, Institutional Care • Family Reunification of Separated/Institutionalised Children • Sociolegal Protection of Child-Headed Households • Aftercare Services for Children in Institutions turning Adults

Child Victims of Violence and Other Problems	Department of Department of Integrated Child Protection	• Rescue & Developing Protective Mechanisms for the Child • Medical & Psychosocial Treatment of Children • Assistance to the Child in the Justice Process • Restorative Justice Services • Family & Community-based Rehabilitation of the Child
Children in Conflict with Law/ Associated with Armed Forces or Armed Groups	Department of Integrated Child Reintegration	• Implementation of the Non-Custodial Community-based Sentences • Assistance to the Child in the Justice Process • Restorative Justice Services • Family & Community-based Reintegration of the Child

Countries around the world have historically focused on institutional care, within as well as outside the juvenile justice system. They used to be called orphanages, although they admitted poor children, living with or without families. Even today, in the developing countries, children that enter the juvenile justice system as children in need of care and protection or as children in conflict with law, are removed from their family and institutionalised. These children could have been helped by supplementary and supportive services.

Institutions cannot provide a family environment and expose children to the same or more deprivation and abuse, and less freedom, than life outside the institutions. Save the Children (2010a) noted that the quality of life for children living in institutions in terms of their development and well-being may be adversely influenced due to reduced potential to form secure, long-lasting attachments, and reduced access to individuals who take a real personal interest in the child's problems and achievements. The institutions are overcrowded and do not provide for privacy. There is reduced or no possibility to maintain contact with family members and friends. The choice of friends, especially from outside the institution, is restricted. Children may face imposition of religious beliefs contrary to their family background. When they leave the institution, they are not prepared for the outside world and their future life. Moreover, they may face stigmatisation in the local community. Save the Children further observed that residential care is an expensive resource; its per capita cost can be twelve times the per capita cost of community-based care options.

According to the UN Guidelines for the Alternative Care of Children (2010), alternatives should be developed in the context of an overall deinstitutionalisation strategy, with precise goals and objectives, which will allow for their progressive elimination. The Guidelines further state that special attention should be paid to use residential care only as a temporary measure until family-based care can be developed; and to prohibit the establishment of new residential facilities structured to provide simultaneous care to large groups of children on a permanent or long-term basis. Save the Children (2010a) noted the challenge that once the institutions are in place, backed by policy, laws and frameworks for the delivery of services, and providing housing and employment, it is difficult to change them and to adapt to new functions in accordance with growing insight into what is best for children even with the argument of it being more expensive.

The focus of the Western countries has been on removal of the abused child from the biological family and placement in foster family care for his/her protection. The substitute services of institutional care, foster family care, and adoption have not only dominated the field of child welfare, their focus on work with the biological family, through the supplementary and supportive child welfare services, has been minimal. The latter services work for family strengthening that helps to maintain children in their own families and prevent removal of children from the family, as well as for children's reunification with the family. There is a dire need to strengthen these services so that child neglect and parent–child separation can be prevented, and children's needs can be met within the family. Because a very small proportion of children live without parental care and the number of orphans is still smaller, substitute childcare should be given a lower priority. Even when it is necessary, it should be for a short term, and all efforts need to be made to strengthen the biological family and reunite the children with them.

Another problem with the child welfare services is the scheme approach that developed as the response to labelling of children by problems. It has led to fragmentation of service delivery in developing countries. The review carried out by the ECPAT International et al. (2014) of national child protection systems in the East Asia and Pacific Region, found that many systems in the past were heavily defined by an emphasis of the international community on such issues as child trafficking, children living on the street, working children, and commercial sexual exploitation. Many child protection systems in these countries continue to bear the influence of short-term project- or issue-based approaches and often reflect donor priorities rather than responding primarily to the holistic needs of children and families. The challenge is that agencies responsible for an issue (such as child labour or child trafficking) tend to establish their own unique subsystems such as separate hotlines, shelters, and referral pathways for a range of categories of children, and databases document the same children but under a different 'issue'. Whereas specialised services and information management systems are necessary, the general perception that emerges from mapping reports is that limited resources are not used effectively.

With the exception of the broadly worded UN Convention on the Rights of the Child, most international standards remain focused on specific child protection issues or categories of children (sexual exploitation, trafficking, labour, child witnesses, children in conflict with the law). An overly compliance-driven approach thus reinforces the development of laws, national action plans, structures, and services to meet international obligations regarding specific categories of children. A related concern is that, given the structure of the CRC reporting and standard template for the CRC Concluding Observations reports, the Committee on the Rights of the Child recommendations are often framed as discrete measures to be taken in relation to a specific category of children (ECPAT International et al., 2014). According to the UN Research Institute for Social Development (UNRISD, 2010), systems that are fragmented, with multiple providers, programmes, and financing mechanisms aimed at different population groups, have limited potential for redistribution, and generally result in high costs, poor quality, and limited access for the poor. As a result of the scheme approach, only symptoms of the problems are addressed but the causes of the problems remained untouched.

3.2.2 Concepts and Review of Child Protection Services

When child abuse was recognised as a problem, the US federal government encouraged states to develop 'protective services' as part of comprehensive child welfare planning. This movement began in the 1950s, and the 1962 amendments to the Social Security Act broadened the definition of 'child-welfare services' to include 'protective services' (Thomas Jr, 1972). UNICEF had focused largely on the basic needs of children in developing countries for a long time. After the legislation of the UNCRC in 1989, that emphasised child protection, UNICEF strengthened its protection capacities throughout the 1990s, for children in especially difficult circumstances.

The emphasis on child protection is leading to diverting resources from preventive supportive and developmental services for children to only for those who are in crisis (Popple & Vecchiolla, 2007). Even in developing countries, when rescue is carried out of child labour or trafficked children, the strategies for rehabilitation of these children with the biological family are weak. It is therefore not surprising that there is a significant degree of recidivism and many children continue to suffer from repeated cycles of maltreatment as a result of return to circumstances of child labour, re-trafficking, abuse, and neglect, etc. (National Commission for Protection of Child Rights, 2010).

According to the Alliance for Child Protection in Humanitarian Action (2019), child protection is the 'prevention of and response to abuse, neglect, exploitation and violence against children'. This definition is now widely used for child protection. However, it includes prevention as well as response and has replaced child welfare in the UNICEF literature as well as in many developing countries, though initially child protection started as a part of child welfare. It is important to note there that the term 'protection' reinforces the adultist notion of children as dependent on adults. If all children are going to be protected for prevention and response, it reinforces adultism. The focus on child protection services therefore needs to be replaced with a comprehensive approach to child welfare, where child protection is one of the child welfare services.

3.2.3 Concepts and Review of Juvenile Justice Systems

Child welfare and protection have been linked to the juvenile justice system which deals with the neglected as well as the offending children. The 'juvenile justice system' is a general term used to describe the policies, strategies, laws, procedures, and practices applied to children over the age of criminal responsibility (UNICEF, 2011). The juvenile justice system has its origin in the late ninetheenth and twentieth centuries when reformers enjoined the child welfare purpose to that of youth correction, by creating the juvenile courts. Their concern was directed towards the youthful lawbreaker and children whose circumstances were likely to lead them into 'delinquency', rather than those who were grossly neglected or in need of other protections (Downs et al., 2009). The major reform achieved by the creation of the juvenile courts in the United States was the removal of child offenders from the criminal courts. However, in regard to the problem of protecting neglected children, the new separate court for children seems to have done little more than confirm and extend the nineteenth-century philosophy of preventive penology, with little thought having been given to the rights of parents and children (Thomas Jr, 1972).

It is important to note that the philosophy of the juvenile justice system has been more or less retributive where the court proceedings often provoke stress for a child. Lack of confidentiality and insensitive treatment by law enforcement agencies, medical and social investigators, and the courts are the main court-related problems due to which child victims do not come forward (UNICEF, 2004). Abused and exploited children go through repeated trauma at the police stations, at hospitals, and in courts in the absence of child-friendly legal procedures and support systems. This is secondary victimisation, which is defined as the victim-blaming attitudes, behaviour, and practices engaged in by community service providers, which results in additional trauma for children, as the negative social or societal reaction or consequence of the primary victimisation. Thus, secondary victimisation of children can be the result of the (wrongful) responses of individuals or institutions to the victim, such as inappropriate language or handling by medical/legal personnel or by other organisations with which the victim has contact after suffering exploitation/abuse. It can also be the result of a treatment that does not correspond to the principles of child-friendly justice, such as repeated police/court hearings, repeated health controls, etc., by multiple persons during the judicial process (ECPAT International, 2016).

According to the WHO (2020), 'secondary victimisation' of children happens through inadequate response of institutions and individuals such as when first-line responders are dismissive, judgmental, or skeptical of their story; children are asked to describe the incident repeatedly while receiving services and accessing justice; children's privacy and confidentiality are not protected; and as a result, they invest excessive time and effort accessing services and justice.

It is important that children who are neglected, who need supplementary or supportive services, should be prevented from entering the juvenile justice system. Similarly, status offenders and children who commit pretty crimes, should be prevented from entering this retributive system. We discussed earlier that 'juvenile delinquency', especially with reference to status offences, is socially constructed and children who commit these offences are criminalised just because of their age. The status offenders should also be prevented from entering the juvenile justice system. According to UNODC (2013), no child shall be arrested, prosecuted, or held criminally responsible for the commission of an act or behaviour that is not considered a criminal offence if committed by an adult. Save the Children (2005) believed that it is vital to decriminalise status offences. They 'recommend that':

i. Survival behaviour such as begging and vagrancy and status offences such as truancy, running away from home and breaching curfews, for example, should be decriminalised. Children should simply not be criminalised for trying to survive, instead they should be supported.
ii. The criminal system should never be used to deal with children who have care issues or are deprived of good parental care for whatever reason. In particular, detention facilities such as remand homes should never be used in such cases.
iii. Children who have not committed a criminal offence but whose behaviour is deemed socially unacceptable should never be dealt with through the justice system.
iv. Children who are victims of violence should never be criminalised (or deprived of their liberty), including children who are trafficked, children in commercial sexual exploitation, children who have been sexually abused, children fleeing forced marriages or who have married without the consent of their parents and eloped.

Moreover, Save the Children (2005) stated that the overwhelming majority of these children (over 90 per cent) are petty offenders, who mainly commit offences against property and four out of five children who commit an offence only commit one in their lifetime. That the overwhelming majority of children in jail are accused of non-serious and non-violent offences point to a fundamental flaw in the way juvenile justice is administered.

A focus on community-based diversion and alternatives to detention for children who have committed petty offences, can free the system and its resources from a backlog of petty offending by children that is only made worse by the use of incarceration, as this is shown to usually lead to more serious offending by young people. Resources and priorities must be refocused away from an expensive, ineffective, and often-dangerous criminal justice system to developing a range of sustainable and localised community-based options focused on reintegration, guidance, and support. The formal criminal justice system should only deal with the small minority of children who have committed profoundly serious crimes, usually involving violence, and who represent a threat to themselves and/or their society (Save the Children, 2005).

Another problem with the juvenile justice system is that the title uses the term 'juvenile' which has the connotation of 'delinquency'. The system therefore stigmatises all the children who are covered by it. It may more appropriately use the word 'child' rather than 'juvenile' as it covers both the categories. There is a need to change the nomenclature of this system to 'justice systems for children' and its scope to cover crimes against children and violent crime by children.

3.2.4 Conclusion

This section reviews the limitations of the current service delivery approaches in child welfare and justice. When referred to the Universal Comprehensive and Longitudinal Conceptual Framework for Problems in Childhood, we can note that there are no services provided at present for preventing children's vulnerability. Services for poor and neglected children are fragmented and dealt with by the juvenile justice system. Neglect of family-strengthening services and focus on institutional substitute childcare, puts children into a situation worse than they were in when outside the institution. Children without parental care are smallest in number and yet, substitute childcare services are largest in number. Supplementary care and support services need to be strengthened. The focus on child protection services for child abuse and commercial exploitation of children needs to be replaced with a comprehensive approach to child welfare, where child protection is one of the child welfare services.

Justice services are necessary for child protection services. The retributive approach of the juvenile justice system has further victimised children, instead of providing justice to them. Due to these limitations, the current service delivery for child welfare and justice have not been effective in breaking the cycle of problems in childhood. There is a need to change the nomenclature of this system to 'justice systems for children', prevent neglected children and status offenders from entering it, and cover only crimes against children and crimes by children.

3.3 Conceptual Framework of Rights-Based, Comprehensive, Preventive, and Systemic Child Welfare

3.3.1 Child Rights-Based Approach

The Preamble of the UN Convention on the Rights of the Child (UNCRC, 1989) noted that the Convention is needed because 'the child, by reason of his physical and mental immaturity, needs special safeguards and care, including appropriate legal protection, before as well as after birth'. It also states that, 'in all countries in the world, there are children living in exceptionally difficult conditions, and that such children need special consideration ... international cooperation for improving the living conditions of children in every country, in particular in the developing countries'.

The UNCRC (1989) implies the following classification of child rights:

i. Child's Development Rights cover health and nutrition, education, and rest and recreation.

ii. Child's Family Rights comprise growing up in a family, parenting by both parents, not to be separated from parents, and reunification with parents, democratic family and societal structure, and family right to assistance for childcare.

iii. Child's Protection Rights cover protection from vulnerability, neglect, abuse, commercial exploitation, conflict with law, and association with armed conflict.

iv. Child's Participation Rights comprise child right to express views, being heard and being given due weight, seek, receive, and impart information, and freedom of thought, conscience, and religion.

According to Article 1 of the UNCRC, 'a child means every human being below the age of eighteen years unless under the law applicable to the child, majority is attained earlier.' A criticism of this age threshold is that with the extension of childhood to age eighteen, more persons are considered children, who have to face adultism as well as the notion of childhood as innocent, asexual, financially illiterate, and apolitical. There is a need to consider adolescence as a stage of transition between childhood and adulthood, rather than a stage within childhood. Another problem with this definition of children covering zero to eighteen years is conceptualisation of children as an age-wise homogenous group. The UNCRC focuses on children rather than childhood as a life stage, implying that children are a never-changing separate group. A life-cycle approach is needed to understand childhood as a life stage, the experiences of which have a bearing on future phases. Moreover, rights in adolescence need to be dealt with differently than those in childhood.

Wyness et al. (2004) criticised the UNCRC (1989) for locating children as welfare dependents. To prevent adultism, more importance needs to be given to the child participatory approach for the recognition of children's entitlement to the right to equal concern and respect as adults. White (2003) noted that the rights to expression of views, communication of information, and freedom in the UNCRC do not adequately amount to right to participation. These do not deal with the blanket exclusion of children from social, economic, or political processes for which appropriate age for specific responsibilities may be worked out. Ensuring child right to family well-being, development, and protection is an adult-driven process if the child right to participation is not promoted. According to Boyden and Levison (2003, cited in White, 2003), growing up without responsibility is not necessarily the most effective way to promote children's well-being and best interests; and a sense of responsibility develops only with participation.

Wyness et al. (2004) noted that the UNCRC is based on the norms of a 'normal' childhood development, based on Western, white, middle-class, male constructs of normality. UNCRC is transferring these mythical norms of 'normal' childhood to the world's children, a majority of whom are growing up in poverty groups of the developing nations. The transfer of these norms to them makes their life seem deviant, inferior, or pathological (White, 2003). The world's children are then vulnerable to services that control and work on them to attain measures that bring them inside the bands of 'normal' (EU Canada Project, 2003).

In spite of all the criticism of the UNCRC (1989), it has been a useful tool for nations to claim rights for children in the aforementioned categories, based on the following child rights principles: foster and ensure self-respect, dignity, and worth of every child, including those who have disability, are victims of crime, or are in conflict with law; give primary consideration to the best interests of the child, in all actions concerning children; ensure rights of every child without discrimination by age, gender, ethnicity, religion, disability, and class; and make the state as the primary duty-bearers of child rights, legally accountable to meet these rights.

The limitations of the current service delivery approaches to children can be addressed by the rights-based service delivery approaches for children. According to this approach, the focus on institutional substitute childcare services needs to be replaced by the family-strengthening approach. The scheme approach leading to fragmentation of services needs to be prevented by the comprehensive, integrated, systemic approach, through FSCs. Focus on child protection services need to be replaced with comprehensive child welfare services where child protection is one of the services. The adultist approach to children as dependents needs to be countered with the participatory and empowerment-oriented approach. Finally, the retributive justice approach needs to be replaced with the rights-based and restorative justice approach.

3.3.2 Comprehensive and Preventive Approach for Child Welfare

Child welfare means the well-being of children and child welfare services are services that promote the well-being of children. Rights-based child welfare services need to be comprehensive, so a comprehensive conceptual framework of child welfare services. The linkages identified in the children's problems in the universal comprehensive and longitudinal conceptual framework of problems in childhood are divided into three consecutive levels: primary, secondary, and tertiary. The primary level problems are problems due to marginalisation that lead to secondary and tertiary levels of problems if not addressed. The secondary level of problems are problems due to poverty and neglect, that lead to tertiary level of problems if not addressed. The tertiary level problems are sociolegal problems that require the justice system. This framework needs to be used for planning preventive services at primary, secondary, and tertiary levels as follows.

Services for Primary Level Problem of Vulnerability in Childhood:

i. Child Development and Child Empowerment Services

Services for Secondary Level Problems of Poverty and Neglect in Childhood:

i. Supplementary Childcare Services
ii. Child Support Services

Services for Tertiary Level Sociolegal Problems in Childhood:

i. Child Protection Services
ii. Substitute/Alternative Childcare Services
iii. Justice for Children
iv. Child Reintegration Services

The preventive approach is an imperative in the rights-based approach as compared to a reactive approach, which merely deals with social problems as they arise. It is the only way to prevent and break the cycle of problems that children face as this approach is grounded in the ecological perspective, oriented to the future, empowerment-focused, developmental (adapted from Downs et al., 2009), cost-effective, and prevents labelling of children. Desai (2019) uses the public healthcare prevention model to propose a rights-based comprehensive policy approach for children, comprising services at the primary, secondary, and tertiary prevention levels.

The framework on problems in childhood implies that problems of children at the primary level can be prevented with primary prevention services, problems at the secondary level can be prevented by secondary prevention services, and problems at the tertiary level can be prevented by the tertiary prevention services. This means that vulnerability in childhood can be prevented by services of child development and child empowerment. Poverty in childhood can be prevented by poverty eradication for families and financial assistance/ sponsorships for children. Neglect of meeting basic needs of children can be prevented by supplementary childcare services and support services for families and children. Sociolegal problems in childhood can be prevented by services for alternative childcare, child protection, justice for children, and child rehabilitation and reintegration services. See Figure 1 for this comprehensive classification of child welfare services in a pyramid form, indicating the large base of children facing problems at the primary level, and minimum number of children needing tertiary level prevention services, especially if the primary and secondary level services are adequately put in place.

The preventive approach is also necessary to prevent further abuse and commercial exploitation of the same children, effects of abuse and commercial exploitation on mental and physical health of children, and abused and commercially exploited children facing conflict with law. The first-time offenders need to be prevented from committing to more offences, status offenders need to be prevented from becoming property offenders, property offenders need to be prevented from becoming violent offenders, and the cycle of violence needs to

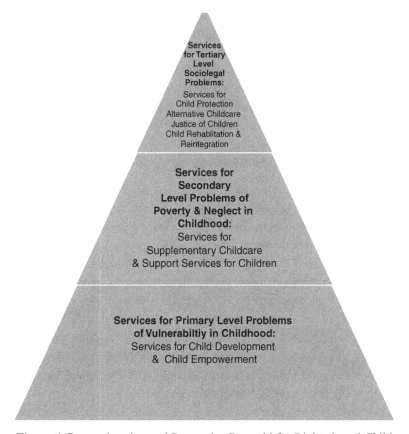

Figure 1 Comprehensive and Preventive Pyramid for Rights-based Child Welfare Services

be curtailed by preventing the victims of violence growing up to be offenders of children as adults.

In moving along the continuum from the primary to the tertiary level, the interventions required become more specialised. As such, they require specific professional support. There can be a degree of overlap between the levels of prevention and this is not a duplication of provision. It reflects a continuum of services required to respond to a wide range of needs. The diversity of childhood and children's situations means that a variety of overlapping services is needed to avoid gaps in provision (Hong, 2007). All levels of intervention can be preventive to some extent: Even at the tertiary level, the aim is to prevent further abuse, exploitation, neglect, or violence as well as initiating processes for children's protection, welfare, and rehabilitation, and avoiding deterioration when circumstances improve.

The primary level services are most effective in groups; however, the secondary as well as the tertiary level services require individualised case management. An important point about primary and the secondary preventive services, is that they are both voluntary. This means that children and families can choose to participate. This optional characteristic contrasts with the tertiary prevention interventions, for which participation is not a choice. The compulsory nature of the tertiary services is the necessary response to a child's situation – a child is already suffering or is highly likely to suffer harm. No matter how effective primary and secondary services are, there will always be a need for high-quality and efficient tertiary services targeted at individual children and their families (Hong, 2007).

3.3.3 Systemic Approach for Child Welfare

In place of the scheme approach that led to fragmentation of services, a comprehensive/integrated systemic approach of service delivery for children has been recommended. In the East Asia and Pacific region, the 2007 UNICEF child protection programming strategy represented a significant shift to a systems approach. The strategy moved investment from issue-specific interventions to strengthening national child protection systems across the region. In 2008, UNICEF endorsed a global child protection strategy, also calling for the strengthening of child protection systems. There is emerging consensus within the international child protection sector on adopting a 'systems approach' to preventing and responding to child maltreatment. In this approach, strengthening a national child protection system is considered a more holistic way of protecting all children (ECPAT International et al., 2014).

Children should first and foremost be seen as whole human beings and not be labelled as a certain category. Because children's problems are interlinked, the policy approach for children has to be integrated to be effective. According to Save the Children (2010b), a 'systems' approach to child protection will need to do the following in addition to ensuring that protection violations and risks that children are exposed to during times of crisis can be responded to quickly and professionally:

i. Work for the protection of all children to address underlying vulnerabilities, rather than targeting individual groups or categories of vulnerable children with disparate initiatives. Children are recognised as people and not just categories.

ii. Address the full range of child protection issues in each context, rather than focusing on one or two 'fundable' concerns.

iii. Make existing child protection structures and interventions more efficient by improving coordination, maximising scarce resources, and eliminating duplication. Because a system is better placed to continually identify and address gaps in child protection in an ongoing way, linking children with a range of services and actors, frequently maximises benefit from finite resources.

Schools are important systems for child welfare at the primary prevention level, and family is important for child welfare at the primary, secondary, as well as the tertiary levels. Integrated Family Service Centres (FSCs) are, therefore, an imperative for comprehensive/integrated/systemic, preventive, and accessible service delivery provisions for children, at the community level. They can provide services to children in the context of families, and in a gender-aware and an inter-generational manner. Community-based FSCs can be planned appropriate to local needs, decentralised, and democratically self-governed. During emergencies, the same centres can provide relief and rehabilitation to victims of emergencies.

The FSCs need to be community-based as community is as important as family. CPWG (2012) emphasised a community-based child protection mechanism (CBCPM), which is a network or group of individuals at community level who work in a coordinated way towards child protection goals. Save the Children (2010b) noted that community-based mechanisms play an important role because they are in proximity to where children and families live. Mobilisation of and support for a network of community mechanisms have potential for significant coverage at scale and may promote long-term sustainability of child rights action. In resource-poor settings and places where the government is unable to fulfil its duties, community mechanisms may support and supplement government capacity. Community mechanisms are important for the functioning of the system and also draw support from the wider system.

Community mechanisms are also key local ways of supporting social transformation, such as changing social norms, beliefs, attitudes, and practices in favour of child rights. Thus, community is the important system to prevent problems for children, protect them, and rehabilitate them.

For tertiary prevention, extended FSCs may be set up at the district level, with Departments for Integrated Alternative Childcare, Integrated Child Protection, and Integrated Child Reintegration services. A protocol needs to be developed for coordination among these centres and departments. These centres may function in coordination with the relevant government, civil society/non-government organisations (NGOs), and international non-government organisations (INGOs), working in the location. These would include the local self-government, NGOs, other civil society organisations such as youth groups, women's groups, senior citizens' clubs, religious organisations, UN organisations, and international NGOs working for children.

3.3.4 Service Delivery Systems for Primary Prevention for All Children

At the primary prevention level, the goals for children may be to prevent all children's vulnerability based in adultism, sexism, ableism, racism, and casteism; and promote children's development and empowerment, through school-based Integrated Child Development and Child Empowerment Services.

Because schools are universal community-based systems for children, besides education, they should provide Integrated Child Development and Child Empowerment Services. Besides education, the child development services that schools should provide are health check-up and first aid services; play, recreation, and cultural activities; library and study centre; facilitation of birth registration certificate and other identity documents; and access to basic needs such as food, shelter, and clothes, etc. The child empowerment services that schools should provide in an integrated manner comprise the following group activities: before/after school for six- to seventeen-year-old children; children's associations, life skills development for children and primary duty-bearers, child rights education for children and primary duty-bearers, family life education and parenting education for parents, etc.

In order to counter the adultist approach to children as dependents, children's participatory approach is essential. Boyden and Levison (2000) opined that children are not merely beneficiaries or passive recipients of adult intervention, or a future societal asset, but social agents in their own right. Supporting children's best interests requires the perspective that they have valid insights into their well-being, valid solutions to their problems, and a valid role in implementing those solutions. Children's agency is a key contributor to their development and hence children should play a part in defining what is in their own best interests. For adults to better understand children's problems and needs, they require children to explain and interpret their childhoods, and only children can provide real insight into their feelings and experiences. Even in adversity, children are active survivors.

Children's participation requires children's empowerment. Children's associations empower children by giving them the opportunity to come together to share their experiences, access information, and analyse issues and power relations that affect them. Facilitating and strengthening children's organisations and networks has been identified as an effective strategy to help children and young people become active citizens by providing them the experience of democracy. In diverse settings across the region, a variety of children's organisations have developed enabling children to unite collectively to work for the realisation of their rights. In their varied organisational forms, children and youth have highlighted a range of child rights issues and injustices, and have made their parents, local communities, media, local and national government officials and institutions take notice of their views and become responsive to injustices in very powerful and transformative ways (Save the Children, 2006).

Life skills comprise self-empowerment, proactive thinking skills, emotional intelligence, and sensitive interpersonal relationship skills. They are empowering as they comprise the components of the empowerment process:

i. Positive perceptions of personal worth, efficacy, and internal locus of control
ii. Recognition, by self and others, that some of one's perceptions about one's self and the surrounding world are indeed valid, and therefore legitimate to voice
iii. The ability to think critically about macro-level social, political and economic systems as well as about one's position within such systems (Torre cited by Parsons, Jorgensen, & Hernandez, 1994).

Article 42 of the UNCRC states that the 'States Parties undertake to make the principles and provisions of the Convention widely known, by appropriate and active means, to adults and children alike.' According to the UNICEF (2015), child rights education is teaching and learning about the provisions and principles of the Convention on the Rights of the Child and the 'child rights approach' – in order to empower both adults and children to take action to advocate for and apply these at the family, school, community, national, and global levels. It helps adults and children work together, providing space and encouragement for the meaningful participation and sustained civic engagement of children. Child rights education comprises education for child rights and responsibilities for participation and children's associations, education, health and hygiene, nutritious food habits, household health and hygiene, prevention of substance abuse, sexual health, environmental health, recreation and mass media literacy, non-discrimination and inclusion, inter-cultural and financial inclusion, etc.

3.3.5 Service Delivery Systems for Secondary Prevention for Poor and Neglected Children

At the secondary prevention level, the goals for poor and neglected children may be to address their problems of poverty and neglect to prevent violence against children, separation from parents, and conflict with law, and their entering the justice systems, through community-based Family Service Centres (FSCs).

FSCs may be set up at the community level, to provide services of poverty eradication for families, financial assistance/sponsorship for children, supplementary childcare, and family and child support services at the secondary prevention level, together with the primary prevention services of child development with reference to preventive health and recreation and cultural activities and child empowerment. The general services to be provided by the FSCs are child helplines for identification of neglected children, community mobilisation, establishing system linkages, creating public awareness on child rights, advocacy for child rights-based policies and programmes, establishing system linkages, training of staff and volunteers, and outcomes-based project cycles. Such FSCs create an empowering, supportive, and protective environment for children, supported by the community and the local self- governance system.

Poor children mostly belong to families in poverty such as those of landless and marginal farmers, migrant and nomadic families, families of unemployed/ unorganised labour, and families living in slums/on the footpath/street. According to the UNICEF and the Global Coalition to End Child Poverty (2017), the policies and programmes to address child poverty should:

> i. Provide quality and accessible services particularly for the most deprived children – including in areas such as nutrition, education and health which represent their multidimensional poverty – and drive whether children will be able to fulfil their potential and end the cycle of poverty; and
>
> ii. Support families and households to have a minimum income and ensure financial barriers do not prevent children from reaching their potential.

The FSCs can provide links to the poor families the employment generation programmes such as food-for-work programmes, employment guarantee schemes, and micro-credit finance schemes, in the community/district. For children, some INGOs are operating child sponsorship programmes, which are based on the concept of a one-to-one relationship between a donor in a developed country and a child in a developing country. Child sponsorship has grown in popularity as it satisfies sponsors' demands for efficacy and psychological benefits, and it secures NGOs' stable revenues for their development goals. A major critique of child sponsorship is around its disrespectful and de-humanising marketing techniques and its individualised service provision which can create conflicts among community members. Faced with these criticisms, some sponsorship NGOs have re-designed child sponsorship to align with community development to address these problems (Noh, 2018).

Child development accounts is another important strategy for not only poor but all children. These are long-term asset-building accounts established for children at birth and allowed to grow over their lifetime. Accounts are typically seeded with an initial deposit and built by contributions from family, friends, and the children themselves. In addition, accounts are augmented by savings matches and other incentives (Howard et al., 2010). According to Beverly, Elliott, and Sherraden (2013), the goal of CDAs is to promote saving and asset building for lifelong development. The CDA assets may be used for postsecondary education for youth and homeownership and enterprise development in adulthood. In many cases, public and private entities deposit funds into these accounts to supplement savings for the child.

Neglected children comprise marginalised children, invisible children, children of families living in poverty, children of single-parent families, children in families with other difficult situations, etc. Support for assistance to families for carrying out their child-rearing responsibilities would help children to grow up in the family, especially when they are in at-risk situations. Childcare together with child support services should address these children's marginalisation, invisibility, poverty, and other difficult situations, and prevent their neglect, abuse, and commercial exploitation, and conflict with law, removal from the family, and entering the justice systems.

Supplementary childcare services provide an extension of parental care or supplement parental care of children. In these services, the main responsibility of childcare rests with the parents and the child continues to live at home most of the time. A UN report's (1956, cited in Kadushin & Martin, 1988) definition of day care is broad enough to cover all the supplementary childcare services: 'an organized service for the care of children away from their own homes during some part of the day when circumstances call for normal care in the home to be supplemented.' The Integrated Supplementary Childcare services to be provided by the FSCs comprise crèches, day/night care/drop-in centres, childcare at homes/family day care, and before/after school care.

The Integrated Child Supportive Services provided through case management aims to support parents and families in performing their care and protection responsibilities, addressing the root causes of the neglect of children. The services included, and not restricted to, are counselling to children and their parents; financial support; legal aid; family reunification of separated children, and linking the families to poverty alleviation and other services; and linking the child to child development services (education, birth registration and health services), child protection, and alternative childcare services. The FSCs should also provide the child empowerment workshops for children and their parents.

3.3.6 Service Delivery Systems for Tertiary Prevention for Children with Sociolegal Problems

At the tertiary prevention level, the goals for children facing sociolegal problems may be to provide sociolegal justice to these children and rehabilitate them – and prevent secondary victimisation and relapse of the same or other problems – through the district-based extended FSCs, in coordination with justice systems for children.

Children with sociolegal problems are children without parental care, child victims of violence, internally displaced children, stateless children, refugee children, children in conflict with law, and children in association with armed conflict. Like the community-based FSCs, the extended FSCs may also provide the following general services for children with sociolegal problems under one umbrella: child helpline, community mobilisation, creating public awareness about and advocacy for child rights, establishing system linkages, training of staff and volunteers, and outcomes-based project cycles. The district-level extended FSCs should also coordinate with community-level FSCs for the primary prevention services of child development and child empowerment and the secondary prevention services of supplementary childcare and child support for rehabilitation of these children. Extended FSCs need to be planned at the district level, with the following departments: Alternative Childcare Department for children without parental care,; Child Protection Department for child victims of violence, internally displaced children, stateless children, and refugee children; and Child Reintegration Department for children in conflict with law. In Western countries, substitute care in the form of foster family care is used for children who are abused by their families. However, in developing countries, substitute care in the form of institutional care is used in varied situations of inadequate parental care. Integrated Alternative Childcare Departments may, therefore, be set up independently of the Integrated Child Protection Departments, though linked to one another.

Details of these services are provided in the following section.

3.4 Summary

This Element's section on Service Delivery Systems for Rights-Based Child Welfare and Justice starts with discussion of the concepts and review of service delivery in this field. With reference to the Universal Comprehensive and Longitudinal Conceptual Framework for Problems in Childhood, we can note that there are no services provided at present for preventing children's vulnerability. Services for poor and neglected children are fragmented and dealt with by the juvenile justice system. Neglect of family strengthening services and focus on institutional substitute childcare, puts children into a situation worse than they were in when outside the institution. Children without parental care represent the smallest percentage of children and yet substitute childcare services are greatest in number. Supplementary care and support services need to be strengthened. The focus on child protection services for child abuse and commercial exploitation of children needs to be replaced with a comprehensive approach to child welfare, where child protection is one of the child welfare services.

Justice services are necessary for child protection services. The retributive approach of the juvenile justice system has further victimised children, instead of providing justice to them. Due to these limitations, the current service delivery systems for child welfare and justice have not been effective in breaking the cycle of problems in childhood. There is a need to change the nomenclature of this system to 'justice systems for children', prevent neglected children and status offenders from entering it, and cover only crimes against children and crimes by children. Due to these limitations, the current service delivery systems for child welfare, protection, and justice have not been effective in breaking the cycle of problems in childhood.

The Element then moves to discuss how the limitations of the current service delivery approaches to children can be replaced by the rights-based, comprehensive, preventive, and systemic service delivery approaches to children. The UNCRC (1989) has been a useful tool for nations to claim rights for children through the child rights-based approach. According to this approach, the focus on institutional substitute childcare services needs to be replaced by the family-strengthening approach. The scheme approach leading to fragmentation of services needs to be prevented by the comprehensive/integrated/systemic approach, through FSCs. Focus on child protection services needs to be replaced with comprehensive child welfare services where child protection is one of the services. The adultist approach to children as dependents needs to be countered with the participatory and empowerment-oriented approach. Finally, the retributive justice approach needs to be replaced with the rights-based and restorative justice approach.

The conceptual framework on problems in childhood leads to a conceptual framework for preventive services for children. It implies that problems of children at the primary level can be prevented with primary prevention services, problems at the secondary level can be prevented by secondary prevention services, and problems at the tertiary level can be prevented by the tertiary prevention services. This means that vulnerability in childhood can be prevented by services of child development and child empowerment. Poverty in childhood can be prevented by poverty eradication for families and financial assistance/sponsorships for children. Neglect of meeting basic needs of children can be prevented by supplementary childcare services and support services for families and children. Sociolegal problems in childhood can be prevented by services for alternative childcare, child protection, justice for children, and child rehabilitation and reintegration services. This comprehensive classification of child welfare services can be perceived in a pyramid form (see Figure 1), indicating the large base of children facing problems at the primary level, and minimum number of children needing tertiary level prevention services, especially if the primary and secondary level services are adequately put in place.

4 Service Delivery Systems for Children with Sociolegal Problems

4.1 Overview

The Element section of Integrated Service Delivery Systems for Children with Socio-Legal Problems goes into the details of these services at the tertiary prevention level. It discusses the service delivery for Integrated Alternative Childcare for children without parental care, Integrated Child Protection for child victims of violence, Integrated Child Welfare for children in emergencies, and Integrated Child Reintegration for children in conflict with law and those associated with armed conflict, through Departments of extended FSCs at the district level.

4.2 Integrated Alternative Care Services for Children without Parental Care

4.2.1 Rights of Children without Parental Care

According to Article 20 of the UNCRC:

1 A child temporarily or permanently deprived of his or her family environment, or in whose own best interests cannot be allowed to remain in that environment, shall be entitled to special protection and assistance provided by the State.

2 States Parties shall in accordance with their national laws ensure alternative care for such a child.

3 Such care could include, inter alia, foster placement, Kafalah of Islamic law, adoption or if necessary, placement in suitable institutions for the care of children. When considering solutions, due regard shall be paid to the desirability of continuity in a child's upbringing and to the child's ethnic, religious, cultural, and linguistic background.

Thus, children without parental care need special protection and assistance through alternative childcare.

4.2.2 Integrated Alternative Childcare Services

Alternative childcare is the care provided for children by caregivers who are not their biological parents (Save the Children, 2013). The UN Guidelines for the Alternative Care of Children (2010) aim to support efforts to keep children in, or return them to, the care of their family or, failing this, to find another appropriate and permanent solution, including adoption and Kafala of Islamic law. To ensure that, while such permanent solutions are being sought, or in cases where they are not possible or are not in the best interests of the child, the most suitable forms of alternative care are identified and provided, under conditions that promote the child's full and harmonious development.

According to the UN Guidelines for the Alternative Care of Children (2010), alternative care may take the form of informal or formal care. Informal Care is any private arrangement provided in a family environment, whereby the child is looked after on an ongoing or indefinite basis by relatives or friends (informal kinship care) or by others in their individual capacity, at the initiative of the child, his/her parents or other person without this arrangement having been ordered by an administrative or judicial authority or a duly accredited body. EveryChild (2011) noted that several risks are associated with informal fostering, in particular, the limited external monitoring of children's well-being and enhanced risk of abuse and exploitation. The obligations of foster carers and the status of children within the family are also ambiguous. It is important to add a degree of formality to such care arrangements to ensure that obligations are clear, and children are well protected. Such problems with informal care are the reason why placement of children in alternative care requires judicial protection and is therefore included at the tertiary prevention level.

Formal Care is all care provided in a family environment which has been ordered by a competent administrative body or judicial authority, and all care provided in a residential environment, including in private facilities, whether or not as a result of administrative or judicial measures (UN, 2010). In the latter situation, children would face similar problems as in informal care due to absence of judicial protection.

Family-based care is a type of alternative care that involves the child living with a family other than his or her biological parents. This is a broad term that can include foster care, kinship care, and supported child-headed households (Save the Children, 2013). In foster care, children are placed by a competent authority for the purpose of alternative care in the domestic environment of a family other than the children's own family that has been selected, qualified, approved, and supervised for providing such care. Kinship care is family-based care within the child's extended family or with close friends of the family known to the child, whether formal or informal in nature (UN, 2010).

Residential or institutional care is care provided in any non-family-based group setting, such as places of safety for emergency care, transit centres in emergency situations, and all other short- and long-term residential care facilities, including group homes (UN, 2010). The SOS Children's Villages are family-like institutions which emphasise family relationships, both between children who live together as brothers and sisters, and between the child and at least one stable, professionally trained, remunerated caregiver: the SOS mother/parent. The organisation also ensures that biological siblings are kept together within one SOS family (SOS-Kinderdorf International, 2008).

A Joint Working Paper on Improving Protection for Children without Parental Care by International Social Service and UNICEF (2004) identified the following areas of concerns with reference to provision of out of home care of children. Foster care and residential placements may be ordered without full consideration of the range of options available (and their specific advantages and disadvantages) and/or without due regard to the needs and circumstances of the individual child. As discussed earlier, unnecessary over-use of residential placements is a common feature of out-of-home care throughout the world because other options have not been developed. Permanency planning is inadequate at present. It should be an integral part of the individualised care plan that needs to be drawn up for each child before or shortly after out-of-home care commences and reviewed regularly as the placement evolves.

Another concern with alternative childcare placement is that inter-country adoption has progressively changed from its initial purpose of providing a family environment for children, to becoming more demand driven. Adoption is not even included as an option in alternative care for children in the UN Guidelines (2010). Increasingly in industrialised countries, inter-country adoption is viewed as an option for childless couples. To meet the demand for children, trafficking flourishes through psychological pressure on vulnerable mothers to give up their children, adoptions organised before birth, false maternity or paternity certificates, abduction of children, children conceived for adoption, and so on (UNICEF, 2004).

The Departments of Integrated Alternative Childcare services in extended FSCs developed at the district level, need to provide the following services for children without parental care to address these concerns through case management: family strengthening and prevention of child-family separation, identification of children without parental care, providing interim residential care and protection to the child, child placement in appropriate alternative childcare with sociolegal protection, family reunification of separated/institutionalised children, sociolegal protection of child-headed households, and aftercare services for children turning adults.

Many placements of children in alternative care could easily be avoided if the major emphasis were to be placed on providing supplementary and support services to enable parents to care for their children themselves. Only in cases of very dysfunctional families with multiple problems, and after all attempts at preventing family breakdowns have been tried, should a child be removed from the parents and placed in alternative care (International Social Service & UNICEF, 2004). Article 9 of the UNCRC emphasises the child right not to be separated from his or her parents, as follows:

1. States Parties shall ensure that a child shall not be separated from his or her parents against their will, except when competent authorities subject to judicial review determine, in accordance with applicable law and procedures, that such separation is necessary for the best interests of the child. . . .
3. States Parties shall respect the right of the child who is separated from one or both parents to maintain personal relationships and direct contact with both parents on a regular basis, except if it is contrary to the child's best interests.

According to the UN Guidelines for the Alternative Care of Children (2010):

i. Removal of a child from the care of the family should be seen as a measure of last resort and should, whenever possible, be temporary and for the shortest possible duration. Removal decisions should be regularly reviewed and the child's return to parental care, once the original causes of removal have been resolved or have disappeared, should be in the best interests of the child.
ii. Financial and material poverty, or conditions directly and uniquely imputable to such poverty, should never be the only justification for the removal of a child from parental care, for receiving a child into alternative care, or for preventing his/her reintegration, but should be seen as a signal for the need to provide appropriate support to the family.'

According to the UN Guidelines for the Alternative Care of Children (2010), in order to prevent abandonment of children by their parents:

> When an agency is approached by a parent or legal guardian wishing to relinquish a child permanently, the State should: 1) ensure that the family receives counselling and social support to encourage and enable them to continue to care for the child. 2) If this fails, other appropriate professional assessment should be undertaken to determine whether there are other family members who wish to take permanent responsibility for the child, and whether such arrangements would be in the best interests of the child. 3) Where such arrangements are not possible or are not in the best interests of the child, efforts should be made to find a permanent family placement within a reasonable period.

The Departments of Integrated Alternative Childcare need to collect information about the following children without parental care at the district level and register them as quickly as possible: children living in their own homes without any adult to care for them as child-headed households, children living on the street without parents, children living in informal alternative care with relatives/friends/neighbours, children living in formal alternative care (foster family care/adoption/institutional care), children growing up in detention centres and prisons, and missing children. According to the International Committee of the Red Cross (2004), identification, registration, and documentation of children without parental care is necessary to promote protection and assistance to these children and the tracing of their families.

The Department of Integrated Alternative Childcare needs to arrange for interim residential care of children without parental care which is care arranged on a temporary basis of up to twelve weeks. The placement may be formal or informal with relatives, foster carers, or in residential care such as interim care centres. The child's care plan should be reviewed every twelve weeks (three months) in order for a longer-term plan and placement to be implemented. After this period, if a child is still in the same care situation, he/she should be referred to as longer-term care (Save the Children, 2013).

According to the UN Guidelines for the Alternative Care of Children (2010), the decision of child placement in alternative childcare should be guided by the principle of the best interests of the child. An underlying principle is that no child should be without the support and protection of a legal guardian or other recognised responsible adult or competent public body at any time. The decision should involve full consultation at all stages with the child, according to his/her evolving capacities, and with his/her parents or legal guardians. The child and his/her parents or legal guardians should be fully informed about the alternative care options available, the implications of each option and their rights and obligations in the matter.

The UN Guidelines for the Alternative Care of Children (2010) further recommend that the decision should be based on assessment of the child and the family's situation and goals for placement. The decision should take full account of the desirability of maintaining the child as close as possible to his/her habitual place of residence, in order to facilitate contact and potential reintegration with his/her family and to minimise disruption of his/her educational, cultural, and social life. Alternative care for young children, especially those under three years of age, should be provided in family-based settings. Siblings with existing bonds should in principle not be separated by placements in alternative care unless there is a clear risk of abuse or other justification in the best interests of the child.

If temporary removal of a child from the care of the biological family is necessary, the child should be placed in alternative family care, such as kinship (extended family) care, or foster family care. In the meantime, the capabilities of the biological families need to be strengthened to care for their children, so that the child can be rehabilitated with his/her family, in the shortest possible duration. Children who need permanent alternative family may be placed in adoption. Institutionalisation of children should be prevented as far as possible and used as the last resort.

All placements in alternative childcare need to follow a legal procedure. According to the UN Guidelines for the Alternative Care of Children (2010), the decision-making on alternative care in the best interests of the child should take place through a judicial, administrative, or other adequate and recognised procedure, with legal safeguards, including, where appropriate, legal representation on behalf of children in any legal proceedings. States should seek to devise appropriate means, consistent with the present Guidelines, to ensure their welfare and protection in informal care arrangements.

The Departments of Integrated Alternative Childcare need to make every effort to facilitate family-child reunification of separated and institutionalised children with the help of supplementary care and support services. The deinstitutionalised children and children who have been rescued from abuse and commercial exploitation, may be reintegrated with their biological families, and if that is not possible, placed in kinship care or foster family care. When the child must be returned to the family from foster family care or institutional care, the child and the family need to be prepared for reunification, especially if the separation has been long (Save the Children, 2004). According to the UN Guidelines for the Alternative Care of Children (2010), the validity of relationships and the confirmation of the willingness of the child and family members to be reunited must be verified for every child.

According to the UN Guidelines for the Alternative Care of Children (2010), support and services should be available to siblings who have lost their parents or caregivers and choose to remain together in their household, to the extent that the eldest sibling is both willing and deemed capable of acting as the household head. States should ensure, including through the appointment of a legal guardian, a recognised responsible adult or, where appropriate, a public body legally mandated to act as guardian, that such households benefit from mandatory protection from all forms of exploitation and abuse, and supervision and support on the part of the local community and its competent services, such as social workers, with particular concern for the children's health, housing, education, and inheritance rights. Special attention should be given to ensuring that the head of such a household retains all rights inherent to his/her child status, including access to education and leisure, in addition to his/her rights as a household head.

The child who is nearing eighteen years of age and who expresses a desire for independent living after discharge from the foster family care or institutional care, needs to be given assistance and sufficient information to help him/her make such a transition. The case manager must facilitate the provision of after-care services for their mainstreaming in society. If the parents are found to be unfit and incompetent, the child shall be placed under an alternative family care. Arrangements for the child's continuing education and medical services, etc. shall be made by the case manager before discharge (adapted from Child Protection Working Group, 2014).

4.3 Integrated Protection Services for Child Victims of Violence

4.3.1 Rights of Child Victims of Violence

According to the Article 19 of the UNCRC (1989):

1. States Parties shall take all appropriate legislative, administrative, social and educational measures to protect the child from all forms of physical or mental violence, injury or abuse, neglect or negligent treatment, maltreatment or exploitation, including sexual abuse, while in the care of parent(s), legal guardian(s) or any other person who has the care of the child.
2. Such protective measures should, as appropriate, include effective procedures for the establishment of social programmes to provide necessary support for the child and for those who have the care of the child, as well as for other forms of prevention and for identification, reporting, referral, investigation, treatment and follow-up of instances of child maltreatment described heretofore, and, as appropriate, for judicial involvement.'

Moreover, Article 39 of the UNRC states that the

States Parties shall take all appropriate measures to promote physical and psychological recovery and social reintegration of a child victim of any form of neglect, exploitation, or abuse; torture or any other form of cruel, inhuman or degrading treatment or punishment; or armed conflicts. Such recovery and reintegration shall take place in an environment, which fosters the health, self-respect, and dignity of the child.

Thus, child victims of violence need legislative, administrative, social, and educational measures for child protection, including effective procedures for the establishment of social programmes for identification, reporting, referral, investigation, treatment, and follow-up as well as judicial involvement .

According to the UN Guidelines on Justice in Matters involving Child Victims and Witnesses of Crime (UN, 2005), child victims and witnesses denote children and adolescents, under the age of eighteen, who are victims of crime or witnesses to crimes regardless of their role in the offence or in the prosecution of the alleged offender or groups of offenders. These UN Guidelines list the following rights of child victims and witnesses of crime in the justice process: The right to be treated with dignity and compassion, the right to be protected from discrimination, the right to be informed, the right to be heard and to express views and concerns, the right to effective assistance, the right to privacy, the right to be protected from hardship during the justice process, the right to safety, the right to reparation, and the right to special preventive measures.

Based on these guidelines, WHO (2018) developed the *INSPIRE Handbook*, where 'child-friendly' systems and services recognise children's right to be treated with dignity and compassion, be given age-appropriate information they can understand, be heard and responded to in a non-judgemental way, receive timely and convenient access to services and procedures, have choice in how care or service is delivered, participate actively in decision making processes, have the opportunity to give informed consent at each step of the care process, be provided procedures adapted for their age and capacity conducted in a child-friendly environment, and have their privacy, confidentiality, integrity, and safety assured.

4.3.2 Integrated Child Protection Services

The district-based Departments of Integrated Child Protection may provide the following services to child victims of violence, through case management: identification and rescue of child victims of violence; providing interim residential care and support to them; initiating protective mechanisms for them; facilitating their disclosure of violence; medical and psychosocial treatment of children; assistance to them in the justice process, and in their family and community-based rehabilitation.

According to the *INSPIRE Handbook* (WHO, 2018), establishing reporting mechanisms allow cases of violence to be officially brought to the attention of relevant authorities. When well publicised and supported by responsive and respectful action by authorities, they help raise public awareness of violence and can strengthen efforts to bring perpetrators of violence to justice. In their regular contact with children and families, social service and health providers may notice potential indications of violence, such as particular types of physical injury, emotional distress, or behavioural problems. Healthcare providers in particular should be alert to the clinical features of child maltreatment and associated risk factors, and consider exposure to child maltreatment when assessing children with conditions possibly caused or complicated by maltreatment, in order to improve identification, diagnosis/identification, and subsequent care, without putting the child at increased risk. Service providers may also recognise signs of family-level risk factors, such as substance misuse, maternal depression, etc. It is true that these signs do not prove violence or maltreatment has occurred. Trained service providers can therefore follow up with clinical inquiry – age-appropriate, child-friendly, and gender-sensitive questions about past or current violence – when they recognise these alerting features. In doing so, care must be taken to avoid blame or stigmatisation (WHO, 2018).

Proper procedures for rapidly identifying child victims of commercial exploitation need to be established. This requires coordination among law enforcement; bus, train, and flight services; hotels; border and immigration authorities; health, education, and non-governmental organisations, all of which should be on the lookout for trafficked children. Rescue operations are needed to remove children from places where they are being exploited, in the form of child labour or child prostitution (adapted from Inter-Parliamentary Union & UNICEF, 2005).

Rescued child victims of violence need interim residential care and protection that include separate safe housing, medical care, education, psychosocial rehabilitation, and reintegration assistance. In identifying appropriate services, attention to a child's cultural identity/origin, gender, age, and such specific needs as disabilities, psychosocial distress, illness, or pregnancy is essential. Special assistance is necessary for children who have been sexually exploited (adapted from Inter-Parliamentary Union & UNICEF, 2005). Priority may be given to place the child with a relative who is competent and willing to keep the child safe and protected. In the absence of a relative, the child may be placed in an accredited child-caring institution, or a foster home.

According to the *INSPIRE Handbook* (WHO, 2018), a child or adolescent should receive the recommended minimum level of first-line support and validation as soon as they disclose violence. The first-line support involves attending to the child in a timely way and in accordance with the child's needs and wishes; ensuring visual and auditory privacy during the encounter; listening respectfully and empathetically, enquiring about the child's worries, concerns, and needs, and answering all questions, offering non-judgmental and validating responses; acting to enhance the child's safety and minimise harms, including those of disclosure and, where possible, the likelihood of further maltreatment; giving age-appropriate information about what will be done to provide care, including whether any disclosure of abuse will need to be reported to relevant designated authorities; and making the environment and manner in which care is provided appropriate to the child's age and sensitive to the needs of those facing discrimination related to, for example, disability or sexual orientation.

According to the *INSPIRE Handbook* (WHO, 2018), studies show that the vast majority of children who experience violence do not tell anyone, let alone seek and receive help. This prevents victims from getting services and accessing justice and leaves them vulnerable to ongoing harm. To facilitate disclosure, it is important to provide information, support, and environments where children feel safe disclosing violence to a trusted adult. The staff needs to be trained to recognise potential signs of violence and provide protocols for clinical inquiry and first-line response, in accordance with international agency guidelines. Efforts to reduce barriers to disclosure, appropriate identification, and reporting mechanisms may increase help-seeking and access to services, improve short- and long-term outcomes for children, and prevent ongoing exposure to violence (WHO, 2018),

Children who have been sexually abused can benefit from non-verbal techniques to facilitate information sharing throughout all stages of the child's care and treatment process. Non-verbal techniques can be used during assessment interviews with child survivors (for example, to help a child share his/her story or clarify specific information) and as part of psychosocial care (by helping children express their feelings through art, play, and other activities). Non-verbal methods of communication offer many benefits. Children may find it easier to express emotions through drawings or stories, especially younger children, and children not used to express emotions or answering questions. Children may feel less threatened using non-verbal methods than sitting in a room talking. Children express emotions, thoughts, ideas, and experiences both during and after the non-verbal communication activity (The International Rescue Committee, 2012).

The *INSPIRE Handbook* (WHO, 2018) recommends that children and other individuals who report violence need to be protected through policies, standards, and procedures that, at a minimum, protect confidentiality and prevent intimidation or retaliation against victims, witnesses, and families; encourage prompt investigation and immediate action, including arrest when appropriate, to ensure children's safety; initiate investigations in cases of violence against children, regardless of whether an official complaint has been filed; remove alleged perpetrators from positions of control or power over the victim or their families; provide for temporary or permanent removal, protection, and care, if required for the child's safety; and enforce restraining orders against alleged offenders.

Child victims of violence need to be treated mentally as well as physically. Abuse and commercial exploitation mainly result in negative emotions in the child, creating guilt, fears, and anxiety, behavioural problems, and lack of trust. Psychosocial intervention is needed to deal with guilt, treat fears and anxiety, treat behavioural problems, and rebuild trust that can be carried out through role-plays and use of the child-case worker relationship. Much of case management practice involves teaching children life skills, mainly self-esteem, problem-solving and assertiveness skills. The case worker can:

i. Help children identify supports in their life, such as friends or family, who can help them in the current situation;

ii. Give practical suggestions for children to meet their own needs (for example, explain how the person can register to receive food aid or material assistance);

iii. Ask the children to consider how they coped with difficult situations in the past, and affirm their ability to cope with the current situation;

iv. Ask the children what helps them to feel better. Encourage them to use positive coping strategies and avoid negative coping strategies (WHO, Wartrauma Foundation, & World Vision, 2011).

Services in the justice systems for children may include raising awareness on the rights of children in the justice systems, promoting child-sensitive procedures and methods; providing legal aid and empowerment to all children, families, and communities; preparing and assisting children in the justice process; preparing the child for the testimony and giving evidence; facilitating restorative justice, etc. Restorative justice is an important reform in the justice systems. According to the UN ECOSOC Resolution (2002) on the basic principles on the use of restorative justice programmes in criminal matters, 'restorative process' means any process in which the victim and the offender, and, where appropriate, any other individuals or community members affected by a crime, participate together actively in the resolution of matters arising from the crime, generally with the help of a facilitator. Restorative processes may include mediation, conciliation, conferencing, and sentencing circles.

Children may be rehabilitated with their families in the community context through the integrated child development, child empowerment, supplementary childcare, and child support services. Depending on the circumstances that brought them there, rescued children often return to the same place because they see no alternative. The rescue of child victims of violence is of no use if they are not given care, treatment, and rehabilitation for a better life than before and are not protected from reoccurrence of the problem.

4.4 Integrated Reintegration Services for Children in Conflict with Law

4.4.1 Rights of Children in Conflict with Law

According to UNICEF (2011), a child 'accused of infringing the penal law' is a term used to refer to children who have been charged with a criminal offence but have not yet been tried before a court. Article 40 of the UNCRC states the following as rights of children accused of conflict with law:

1. State Parties recognize the right of every child alleged as, accused of, or recognised as having infringed the penal law to be treated in a manner consistent with the promotion of the child's sense of dignity and worth, which reinforces the child's respect for the human rights and fundamental freedoms of others . . .
2. b) Every child alleged as or accused of having infringed the penal law has at least the following guarantees:
   i. To be presumed innocent until proven guilty according to law.
   ii. To be informed promptly and directly of the charges against him or her, and, if appropriate, through his or her parents or legal guardians, and to have legal or other appropriate assistance in the preparation and presentation of his or her defence.
   iii. To have the matter determined without delay by a competent, independent, and impartial authority or judicial body in a fair hearing according to law.
   iv. Not to be compelled to give testimony or to confess guilt; to examine or have examined adverse witnesses and to obtain the participation and examination of witnesses on his or her behalf under conditions of equality.
   v. If considered to have infringed the penal law, to have this decision and any measures imposed in consequence thereof reviewed by a higher competent, independent, and impartial authority or judicial body according to law.

vi. To have the free assistance of an interpreter if the child cannot understand or speak the language used.

vii. To have his or her privacy fully respected at all stages of the proceedings.

According to UNICEF (2011), a convicted child is a child who has been found guilty of a criminal offence by a court exercising criminal jurisdiction. As far as rights of convicted children is concerned, according to Article 37 of the UNCRC: States Parties shall ensure that:

(a) No child shall be subjected to torture or other cruel, inhuman, or degrading treatment or punishment. Neither capital punishment nor life imprisonment without possibility of release shall be imposed for offences committed by persons below eighteen years of age.

(b) No child shall be deprived of his or her liberty unlawfully or arbitrarily. The arrest, detention or imprisonment of a child shall be in conformity with the law and shall be used only as a measure of last resort and for the shortest appropriate period of time.

(c) Every child deprived of liberty shall be treated with humanity and respect for the inherent dignity of the human person, and in a manner, which takes into account the needs of persons of his or her age. In particular, every child deprived of liberty shall be separated from adults unless it is considered in the child's best interest not to do so and shall have the right to maintain contact with his or her family through correspondence and visits, save in exceptional circumstances;

(iv) Every child deprived of his or her liberty shall have the right to prompt access to legal and other appropriate assistance, as well as the right to challenge the legality of the deprivation of his or her liberty before a court or other competent, independent and impartial authority, and to a prompt decision on any such action.'

4.4.2 Integrated Child Reintegration Services

Departments of Integrated Child Reintegration may be set up for children in conflict with law in the extended FSCs at the district level. According to UNICEF (2004), there is a need for effective programmes that help adolescents involved in crime overcome their problems, to the extent possible, and assist them in preparing for life as law-abiding members of society. Large numbers of children who are in conflict with the law need to be diverted from formal criminal justice processes into correction programmes which challenge their offending behaviour at the same time as allowing them to remain living with their families in the community.

Save the Children (2012) recommends that Community-based Correction Centres may have the following preventive objectives:

i. Prevent potentially vulnerable children from being involved in criminal activities.
ii. Keep young offenders at home not in reformatory institutions.
iii. Help young people avoid the trauma and stigma associated with involvement in the formal justice process and help them avoid a criminal record.
iv. Reduce the likelihood of future criminal involvement through targeted and individualised rehabilitation; and
v. Increase collaboration between police stations and local communities in crime prevention for children.

The UNODC (2013) recommended that specialised police units shall be established in each police station, where only designated and specially trained child police officers shall work. Where there are no specialised police units for children, specialised police officers shall be nominated to deal exclusively with child offenders. The UNODC also recommended that specialised child prosecution offices shall be established by law in each court district. Where there is no specialised child prosecution office, a specialised child prosecutor shall be nominated to deal exclusively with child offenders.

The UNODC (2013) recommended the following rights of the child during the trial: right to legal assistance, right to fair and speedy trial, right to information prior to trial, restrictions on the use of handcuffs and other restraints, right to presence of parents or legal guardian during trial, right to legal aid and consular assistance during trial, right to participation during trial, and right to hear evidence during trial.

According to UNODC (2013), the purpose of a sentence imposed on a child by the children's court shall be to promote the rehabilitation and reintegration of the child into society. The UNODC recommended that every children's court that imposes a sentence on a child found guilty of a criminal offence shall take into account the following principles:

i. The child is to be dealt with in a manner appropriate to his or her well-being.
ii. Any sentence given to the child must be proportionate not only to the circumstances and the gravity of the offence but also to his or her age, individual circumstances and needs.
iii. Any sentence must promote the reintegration of the child and his or her assumption of a constructive role in society.
iv. The sentence imposed must be the one most likely to enable the child to address his or her offending behaviour.

v. The sentence must be the least restrictive one possible.

vi. Detention is a measure of last resort and must not be imposed unless all available sentences other than a custodial sentence have been considered and adjudged inappropriate to meet the needs of the child and provide for the protection of society; and

vii. Following every conviction, an individual sentencing plan must be elaborated.

According to UNODC (2013), where a child is convicted of a criminal offence, the children's court shall consider, having regard to the circumstances of the case, alternatives to detention. The children's court shall have the power to order more than one non-custodial measure and to determine whether such sentences should run concurrently or consecutively.

The Department of Integrated Child Reintegration may implement the non-custodial sentences such as attendance at a community-based programme to help the child address his or her offending behaviour, intermediate treatment and other treatment orders, probation, a restorative justice order, a drug or alcohol treatment order, attendance at counselling, a community service order, an education order, an exclusion order, a curfew order, a prohibited activity order, a supervision order, an intensive supervision order, a short-term fostering order, a residence order, a care order, a suspended sentence, etc. (UNODC, 2013).

Save the Children (2005) noted that regulating conditions of detention is a fundamental requirement for preventing violence, including ensuring the segregation of children away from adults, the separation of boys from girls, and the convicted from those awaiting trial. The investigation and prosecution of perpetrators of violence and those who abuse the system, including officials responsible for condoning arbitrary and unlawful detention, should be a priority for governments. In case of conviction, the criminal record of a child's offence-(s) shall be kept strictly confidential and closed to third parties. The record shall not be used in adult proceedings involving the same child (UNODC, 2013).

The juvenile justice system is not well equipped to screen, assess, or treat a young person who has special mental, emotional, or behavioural needs. Incarceration presents potential risks for these children, including victimisation, self-injury, and suicide. For these reasons, children should be diverted from incarceration whenever possible with community-based alternatives. Moreover, these children need treatment for their disorders, and the correctional facilities and programmes should have adequate policies and procedures for identifying and treating these youth. Children who need help must be identified before their behaviours escalate and/or create problems for the authorities (National Mental Health Association, 2004).

Children in conflict with law may be provided assistance in the justice process by providing legal aid, providing all relevant information, namely, information about the justice process, preparing the child for giving testimony and evidence, accompanying the child to the police station and the court, facilitating restorative justice, etc. In the restorative model, children are not understood as criminal elements or a threat to social order. They are, instead, acknowledged as members of a community, and that community assumes responsibility for them, just as they, the children, assume responsibility for the offences they have committed and pledge to restore the harm they may have caused (SRSG on Violence against Children, 2013). The SRSG report on Violence against Children (2013) has identified the following benefits of restorative justice for child offenders: taking responsibility and changing behaviour, feeling respected and being heard during the restorative justice process, avoiding the harmful effects of deprivation of liberty, and freedom from stigma.

Children may be reintegrated with their families and communities through the integrated child development, child empowerment, supplementary child-care, and child support services. According to the Paris Principles (2007), child reintegration is the process through which children transition into civil society and enter meaningful roles and identities as civilians who are accepted by their families and communities in a context of local and national reconciliation. Sustainable reintegration is achieved when the political, legal, economic, and social conditions needed for children to maintain life, livelihood, and dignity have been secured. This process aims to ensure that children can access their rights, including formal and non-formal education, family unity, dignified livelihoods, and safety from harm. The Paris Principles recommended that to enable children's return and reintegration, it is vital to prepare the family and community and also to provide mediation and support following children's return.

The Paris Principles (2007) note that engaging children in community service and helping them enter respected social roles are essential in breaking stigma and enabling children to develop appropriate support networks in the community. For supporting children in finding a role in their community, they recommend that:

i. Programmes should recognise and build upon the skills and confidence that girls and boys may have learned while associated with the armed force or armed group. This will entail creating options and choices for them, so that they are not channelled into inappropriate or de-skilling training or livelihood options.

ii. In particular, adolescent boys and girls need to be recognised for their particular capacities and resilience as well as their vulnerabilities. Their full participation should be included in the assessment, design, and implementation of programmes. Engaging children in community service and helping them enter respected social roles are essential in breaking stigma and enabling children to develop appropriate support networks in the community.

iii. Reintegration and reconciliation activities should recognise the need to redirect the potential of children and young people in developing leadership and conflict resolution skills and taking responsibility for their actions including through participation in the rebuilding of their communities and in peace building activities. Programmes that involve women's organisations can be particularly useful in this regard with girls who need both positive role models and a supportive environment.

4.5 Integrated Welfare Services for Children in Emergencies

4.5.1 Rights of Children during Emergencies

Rights of children during emergencies are drawn from the Principles of Humanitarian Action and the Children's Charter for Disaster Risk Reduction. The IASC (2007) recommended the following principles of humanitarian action: human rights and equity, participation, building on available resources and capacities, integrated support systems, and multi-layered supports.

Recognising the impact of disasters on children and their role in risk reduction, the Children's Charter for Disaster Risk Reduction (DRR) which identified children's priorities for risk reduction, was launched at the Global Platform in 2011 by Plan International, Save the Children, UNICEF and World Vision. The Charter was developed through consultations with over 600 children in 21 high-risk countries in Africa, Asia, and Latin America and identified 'five key priorities for child-centred DRR':

i. Schools must be safe, and education must not be interrupted.

ii. Child protection must be a priority before, during and after a disaster.

iii. Children have the right to participate and to access the information they need.

iv. Community infrastructure must be safe, and relief and reconstruction must help reduce future risk.

v. DRR must reach the most vulnerable. (Children in a Changing Climate, 2013)

Five focus areas have been identified under this Charter:

i. Inclusion of child protection risks in disaster risk assessments and targeting of high-risk areas with interventions designed to strengthen the resilience of the most vulnerable children and families.
ii. Strengthening existing child protection systems so that responsible actors are able to prepare for and respond to disasters.
iii. Provision of life saving knowledge and skills for girls, boys, families, and communities, including the most vulnerable children in a particular context, such as disabled children, street children, working children, or others.
iv. Provision of birth registration identification (ID) and other forms of ID made available and kept safe from potential hazards.
v. Ensuring that adequate laws, policies, and mechanisms are in place and are adequately resourced to ensure implementation at national and local levels to safeguard appropriate care and protection for children during emergencies. (Children in a Changing Climate, 2013)

4.5.2 Integrated Child Welfare Services

During emergencies, the district-based extended FSC may set up a special Department of Integrated Child Welfare that needs to provide the following specific services during emergencies: strengthen the service systems for children; provide primary prevention services to all children, namely, integrated child development and child empowerment services; identify neglected children and provide them secondary prevention services, namely, supplementary childcare and support services; and identify children facing sociolegal problems and provide them tertiary prevention services, namely, child protection, alternative childcare, and child reintegration services.

The Departments of Integrated Child Welfare may plan their functioning during emergencies based on the Principles of Humanitarian Action and the Children's Charter for DRR. These Departments should strengthen the core systems for children, namely, schools, community-based FSCs, and the justice systems for children, to provide services for children at the primary, secondary, and tertiary levels.

At the primary prevention level, children in emergencies may be provided psychological first aid (PFA), and Integrated Child Development and Child Empowerment Services. These activities maybe provided through schools or, if schools have closed down during the emergency, child-friendly spaces (CFS) may be set up in an existing safe structure to provide integrated child development and child empowerment services, such as facilitating children's associations and providing life skills development and child rights education.

Psychological first aid (PFA) is also an important approach to all children during emergencies. According to the WHO et al. (2011), a person in distress can feel overwhelmed with worries and fears. PFA is important to him/her as it is a humane, supportive response to a fellow human being who is suffering and who may need support. PFA involves the following themes: providing practical care and support, which does not intrude; assessing needs and concerns; helping people to address basic needs (for example, food and water, information); listening to people, but not pressuring them to talk; comforting people and helping them to feel calm; helping people connect to information, services, and social supports; helping them to consider their most urgent needs, and how to prioritise and address them; and protecting people from further harm. WHO et al. also identified that PFA is not something that only professionals can do: it is not professional counselling, it is not 'psychological debriefing' in that PFA does not necessarily involve a detailed discussion of the event that caused the distress, and it is not asking someone to analyse what happened to them or to put time and events in order.

According to the CPWG (2012, p. 149):

> child-friendly spaces (CFS) mean safe spaces where communities create nurturing environments in which children can access free and structured play, recreation, leisure, and learning activities. CFSs may provide educational and psychosocial support and other activities that restore a sense of normality and continuity. They are designed and operated in a participatory manner, often using existing spaces in the community. Different agencies call CFSs different things – safe spaces, child centred spaces, child protection centres or emergency spaces for children. (Global Education Cluster, Global Protection Cluster, INEE, & Inter-Agency Standing Committee, 2011)

CFSs are widely used in emergencies as a first response to children's needs and an entry point for working with affected communities. Because CFSs can be established quickly and respond to children's rights to protection, psychosocial well-being, and non-formal education, CFSs are typically used as temporary supports that contribute to the care and protection of children in emergencies. However, they are used also as transitional structures that serve as a bridge to early recovery and long-term supports for vulnerable children. Broadly, the purpose of CFSs is to support the resilience and well-being of children and young people through community-organised, structured activities conducted in a safe, child-friendly, and stimulating environment (Global Education Cluster et al., 2011).

According to UNICEF (2018), the main principles of CFSs are that they are secure and safe environments for children, provide a stimulating and supportive environment for children, are built on existing structures and capacities within a community, use a fully participatory approach for the design and implementation, provide or support integrated services and programmes, and are inclusive and non-discriminatory.

At the secondary prevention level, community-based FSCs can set up supplementary childcare and child support services in emergencies, if they do not have those. At the tertiary prevention level, the IASC (2011) recommended that the affected persons should be protected against trafficking, child labour, contemporary forms of slavery such as sale into marriage, forced prostitution, sexual exploitation, and similar forms of exploitation. 'Amongst others the following activities can be considered':

  i. Conducting awareness-raising campaigns targeted towards affected population on the risks of trafficking, exploitation, etc.
 ii. Enrolment of children in formal or informal educational activities or provision of other child-friendly spaces at the earliest moment possible.
iii. Building the capacity of law enforcement agencies on how to investigate and respond to incidences of trafficking, child labour, and similar forms of exploitation.
 iv. Including sufficient trained female staff into law enforcement activities, either through fast-track recruitment or involvement of the women in the communities.
  v. Setting up, in collaboration with local law enforcement officials, the judiciary and community management committees, of child and women-friendly procedures to enable victims and their families to report incidents of trafficking, child labour, and similar forms of exploitation.
 vi. Conducting, as soon as possible, thorough investigations and prosecution of perpetrators of trafficking, child labour, recruitment of children, and similar forms of exploitation; as well as effective victim and witness protection. (IASC, 2011)

4.6 Summary

The Element section of Integrated Service Delivery Systems for Children with Sociolegal Problems goes into the details of these services that may be provided by departments set up in the extended FSCs at the district level to provide services for children at the tertiary prevention level.

For children without parental care, the service delivery systems discussed are Departments of Integrated Alternative Childcare that may provide the following services through case management: family strengthening and prevention of child-family separation, identification of children without parental care, providing interim residential care and protection to the child, child placement in appropriate alternative childcare with sociolegal protection, family reunification of separated/institutionalised children, sociolegal protection of child-headed households, and aftercare services for children turning adults.

The Departments of Integrated Child Protection for child victims of violence may provide the following services through case management: identification and rescue of child victims of violence, providing interim residential care and support to the child, initiating protective mechanisms for the child, facilitating child's disclosure of violence, medical and psychosocial treatments, assistance to child victims in the justice process, and rehabilitation of the child with the family in the community context. The rights of child victims and witnesses of crime in the justice process comprise the right to be treated with dignity and compassion, the right to be protected from discrimination, the right to be informed, the right to be heard and to express views and concerns, the right to effective assistance, the right to privacy, the right to be protected from hardship during the justice process, the right to safety, the right to reparation, and the right to special preventive measures.

The services of Departments of Integrated Child Reintegration for children in conflict with law may comprise implementation of the non-custodial community-based orders, assessment and treatment of children with special needs in conflict with law, assistance to children in conflict with law in the justice process, facilitating restorative justice for children in conflict with law, and reintegration of the children with the family and the community.

The district level FSCs may adapt their functioning during emergencies or start a new department for children in emergencies. If needed, more such centres may be set up in affected communities. These Departments should strengthen the core systems for children. It may ensure that all children facing emergencies may receive primary prevention services of integrated child development and child empowerment; poor and neglected children receive secondary prevention services, namely, supplementary childcare and support services; and children facing sociolegal problems receive tertiary prevention services, namely, child protection, alternative childcare, and child rehabilitation services.

Service delivery systems for children with sociolegal problems discussed in this section draw heavily from emerging guidelines by the UN and children's INGOs, which are developed in consultation with work on the ground in different countries. However, unless the primary and secondary level service delivery systems are strong, tertiary level service delivery systems will continue to face problems of understanding, implementation, and outcome. In other words, inadequate understanding of social construction of childhood, half-hearted implementation of poverty eradication, domination of child protection, juvenile justice system and its institutional services, and absence of comprehensiveness, prevention, and systemic approach, are major constraints in service delivery of the international guidelines at the tertiary level.

References

The Alliance for Child Protection in Humanitarian Action. (2019). *Minimum standards for child protection in humanitarian action*. https://alliancecpha .org/en/CPMS_home

Beverly, S. G., Elliott, W., & Sherraden, M. (2013). *Child development accounts and college success: Accounts, assets, expectations, and achievements*. CSD Perspective, 13–27.

Bhasin, K. (2000). *Understanding gender*. Kali for Women.

Boyden, J., & Levison, D. (2000). *Children as economic and social actors in the development process*. Ministry of Foreign Affairs, Sweden.

Brewer, D. (2008). *Globalization and human trafficking*. www.du.edu/korbel/ hrhw/researchdigest/trafficking/Globalization.pdf

Burman, E. (2008). *Deconstructing developmental psychology* (2nd ed.). Routledge Taylor and Frances Group.

Child Protection Working Group. (2012). *Minimum standards for child protection in humanitarian action*. http://cpwg.net/wp-content/uploads/2013/08/ CP-Minimum-Standards-English-2013.pdf

Child Protection Working Group. (2014). *Protocol for case management of child victims of abuse, neglect, and exploitation*. http://cpwg.net/wp-content/ uploads/sites/2/2014/05/Philippines-CSPC-protocol.pdf

Child Welfare Information Gateway. (2014). *Definitions of child abuse and neglect*. www.childwelfare.gov/pubPDFs/define.pdf

Child Welfare Information Gateway. (2019). *What is child abuse and neglect? Recognizing the signs and symptoms*. www.childwelfare.gov/pubPDFs/wha tiscan.pdf#page=2&view=How%20is%20child%20abuse%20and%20neg lect%20defined%20in%20Federal%20law?

Children in a Changing Climate. (2013). *Towards the resilient future children want: A Review of progress in achieving the Children's Charter for Disaster Risk Reduction, World Vision UK*. http://9bb63f6dda0f744fa444-9471a7fca5768c c513a2e3c4a260910b.r43.cf3.rackcdn.com/files/5813/7658/5189/Towards_the_ resilient_future_2013_lowres.pdf

Christian Children's Fund (2005). *Understanding children's experience of poverty: An introduction to the DEV framework*. http://citeseerx.ist.psu .edu/viewdoc/download?doi=10.1.1.499.209&rep=rep1&type=pdf

Connelly, P., Li, T. M., MacDonald, M., & Parpart, J. L. (2000). Feminism and development: Theoretical perspectives. In J. L. Parpart, M. P. Connelly, & V. E. Barriteau (Eds.), *Theoretical perspectives on gender and development*.

International Development Research Centre. www.idrc.ca/es/ev-27444–201-1-DO_TOPIC.html

Consortium for Street Children & Plan. (2011). *Still on the street – Still short of rights: Analysis of policy and programmes related to Street Involved Children.* https://childhub.org/en/system/tdf/library/attachments/csc_11_the_streets_0311.pdf?file=1&type=node&id=19067

Corby, B. (2002). Child abuse and child protection. In B. Goldson, M. Lavalette, & J. McKechnie (Eds.), *Children, welfare and the state* (pp. 136–151). Sage Publications.

Department for International Development. (2005). Reducing poverty by tackling social exclusion: A DFID policy paper. http://webarchive.nationalarchives.gov.uk/+/http://www.dfid.gov.uk/Documents/publications/social-exclusion.pdf

Desai M. (2010). *A rights-based preventative approach for psychosocial well-being in childhood,* Series on *Children's Well-Being: Indicators and Research.* Springer.

Desai, M. (2018). *Introduction to rights-based direct practice with children,* A CRY Series of Sourcebooks on *Rights-Based Direct Practice with Children.* Springer Nature.

Desai, M. (2019). *Rights-based integrated service delivery systems for child protection: secondary and tertiary prevention,* A CRY Series of Sourcebooks on *Rights-Based Direct Practice with Children.* Springer Nature.

Downs, S. W., Moore, E., & McFadden, E. J. (2009). *Child welfare and family services: Policies and practice,* (8th ed.). Pearson AandB.

ECPAT. (2006). Protecting children from sexual exploitation & sexual violence in disaster & emergency situations: A guide for local & Community based Organisations, ECPAT International, Bangkok. http://www.preventionweb.net/files/2709_protectingchildren.pdf

ECPAT. (2014). The commercial sexual exploitation of children in South Asia: Developments, progress, challenges and recommended strategies for civil society. www.ecpat.org/wp-content/uploads/2016/04/Regional%20CSEC%20Overview_South%20Asia.pdf

ECPAT International. (2016). Terminology guidelines for the protection of children from sexual exploitation and sexual abuse. Bangkok. http://luxembourgguidelines.org/

ECPAT International, Plan International, Save the Children, UNICEF, & World Vision. (2014). National child protection systems in the East Asia and Pacific Region: A review and analysis of mappings and assessments, Bangkok: ECPAT International. https://resourcecentre.savethechildren.net/library/national-child-protection-systems-east-asia-and-pacific-region-review-and-analysis-mappings

EU Canada Project. (2003). *Child welfare across borders.* www.sws.soton.ac .uk/cwab/index.htm

EveryChild. (2011). Fostering better care: Improving foster care provision around the world. Positive care choices: Working paper 2. www.crin.org/ docs/FosteringBetterCare

Gallacher, L., & Kehily, M. J. (2013). Childhood: A sociocultural approach. In M. J. Kehily (Ed.), *Understanding Childhood: A cross-disciplinary approach* (2nd ed., pp. 211–266). The Polity Press.

Global Education Cluster, Global Protection Cluster, INEE, & Inter-Agency Standing Committee. (2011). *Guidelines for child friendly spaces in emergencies.* www.unicef.org/protection/Child_Friendly_Spaces_Guidelines_for_ Field_Testing.pdf

Griffin, S. (2008). *Inclusion, equality and diversity in working with children.* Pearson Education Limited.

Hess, K. M., & Drowns, R.W. (2004). *Juvenile justice.* Thomson Wadsworth.

Hong, S. (2007). *Child protection programme strategy toolkit.* UNICEF East Asia and Pacific Regional Office. www.unicef.org/eapro/Protection_Tool kit_all_Parts.pdf

Howard, R., Humphrey, L., Rist, C., Rosen, B., & Tivol, L. (2010). *From piggy banks to prosperity: A guide to implementing children's savings accounts.* SEED. http://cfed.org/assets/pdfs/Piggy_Banks_to_Prosperity.pdf

An Interagency Modular Training Package. (2008). *Introduction to child protection in emergencies.*

Inter-Agency Standing Committee. (2007). *IASC guidelines on mental health and psychosocial support in emergency settings.* Geneva. www.who.int/ mental_health/emergencies/guidelines_iasc_mental_health_psychosocial_ june_2007.pdf

Inter-Agency Standing Committee. (2011). *IASC operational guidelines on the protection of persons in situations of natural disasters,* The Brookings-Bern Project on Internal Displacement. https://docs.unocha.org/sites/dms/ Documents/Operational%20Guidelines.pdf

International Bureau for Children's Rights. (2010). *Children and armed conflict: A guide to international humanitarian and human rights law.* Montreal: Author. www.essex.ac.uk/armedcon/story_id/000911.pdf

International Committee of the Red Cross. (2004). *Inter-agency guiding principles on unaccompanied and separated children.* Geneva: Author. www .unicef.org/protection/IAG_UASCs.pdf

International Labor Organization. (2008). *Commercial sexual exploitation of children and adolescents The ILO's response.* www.ilo.org/ipec/WCMS_100740/ lang–en/index.htm

International Labour Organization (n.d.). *What is child labour.* www.ilo.org/ipec/facts/lang–en/index.htm

International Rescue Committee. (2012). *Caring for child survivors of sexual abuse: Guidelines for health and psychosocial service providers in humanitarian settings.* Author. www.unicef.org/pacificislands/IRC_CCSGuide_FullGuide_lowres.pdf

International Social Service & United Nations Children's Fund. (2004). *Joint working paper on improving protection for children without parental care: a call for international standards.* Geneva. www.crin.org/docs/resources/treaties/crc.40/GDD_2005_CALL_FOR_INT_STANDARDS.pdf

Inter-Parliamentary Union & United Nations Children's Fund. (2005). *Combating child trafficking.* www.unicef.org/ceecis/IPU_combattingchildtrafficking_GB.pdf

James, A., & James, A. (2004). *Constructing childhood: Theory, policy and social practice.* Palgrave Macmillan.

James, A., & James, A. (2012). *Key concepts in childhood studies* (2nd ed.). Sage.

Jans, M. (2004). Children as citizens: Towards a contemporary notion of child participation. *Childhood, 11*(1), 27–44.

Jones, G. (2009). *Youth.* Polity Press.

Kadushin, A., & Martin, J. A. (1988). *Child welfare services* (4th ed.). Macmillan Publishing. http://linc.nus.edu.sg:2084/record=b1220699

Koramoa, J., Lynch, M. A., & Kinnair, D. (2002). A continuum of child-rearing: Responding to traditional practices. *Child Abuse Review*, 11(6), 415–421.

Korbin, J. E. (2003). Children, childhoods, and violence. *Annual Review of Anthropology, 32*, 431–446.

Le Francois, B. (2013). Adultism. www.researchgate.net/publication/280102266_Adultism

Lesser, J. G., & Pope, D. S. (2007). *Human behavior and the social environment: Theory and practice.* Pearson Allyn and Bacon.

Levison, D. (2000). Children as economic agents. *Feminist Economics, 6*(1), 125–134. www.tandfonline.com/doi/abs/10.1080/135457000337732

Mitlin, D., & Hickey, S. (2009). Introduction. In D. Mitlin & S. Hickey (Eds.), *Rights-based approach to development: Exploring the potential and pitfalls* (pp. 3–20). Kumarian Press.

The National Center on Education, Disability and Juvenile Justice. (n.d.). *Resources on prevention of delinquency.* www.edjj.org/focus/prevention/

National Commission for Protection of Child Rights. (2010). *Protocols for police and armed forces in contact with children in areas of civil unrest.* http://ncpcr.gov.in/view_file.php?fid=464

National Mental Health Association. (2004). *mental health treatment for youth in the juvenile justice system: A compendium of promising practices*. www .nmha.org/children/JJCompendiumofBestPractices.pdf.

Noh, J. E. (2018). *Human rights-based child sponsorship: A case study of ActionAid*. https://doi.org/10.1007/s11266-018-0010-2

Parsons, R. J., Jorgensen, J. D., & Hernandez, S. H. (1994). *The integration of social work practice*. Brooks/Cole Publishing Company.

The Paris Principles. (2007). *Principles and guidelines on children associated with armed forces or armed groups*. www.unicef.org/mali/media/1561/file/ParisPrinciples.pdf

Pinheiro, S. (2006). *World report on violence against children*. Geneva. www .unicef.org/lac/full_tex(3).pdf

Popple, P. R., & Vecchiolla, F. (2007). *Child welfare social work: An introduction*. Pearson/Allyn and Bacon.

The Power of Labelling in Development Practice. (2006). *IDS Policy Briefing, 28*.

Ruddick, S. (2003). The politics of aging: Globalization and the restructuring of youth and childhood. *Antipode: A Radical Journal of Geography, 35*(2), 334–362.

Save the Children. (2004). *Separated children: Care & protection of children in emergencies: A field guide*. https://resourcecentre.savethechildren.net/sites/default/files/documents/2692.pdf

Save the Children. (2005). *The right not to lose hope: Children in conflict with the Law*. London: Author. https://resourcecentre.savethechildren.net/node/3128/pdf/3128.pdf

Save the Children. (2006). Children and young people as citizens: Partners for social change: 2 Learning from experience. Sweden: Author. http://resource centre.savethechildren.se/library/children-and-young-people-citizens-part ners-social-change-learning-experience-part-2

Save the Children. (2009). Allies for change: Together against violence and abuse working with boys and men: A discussion paper for programmers and practitioners. Sweden: Author.

Save the Children. (2010a). *A Last Resort: The Growing Concern about Children in Residential Care*. Author. www.savethechildren.org.uk/sites/default/files/docs/A_last_resort_1.pdf

Save the Children. (2010b). *Strengthening national child protection systems in emergencies through community-based mechanisms: A discussion paper*. http://childprotectionforum.org/wp/wp-content/uploads/downloads/2012/05/Community-mechanisms-in-emergencies.pdf

Save the Children. (2012). *Child protection and child friendly justice: Lessons learned from programmes in Ethiopia: Executive summary*. Addis Ababa:

Author. http://resourcecentre.savethechildren.se/sites/default/files/docu ments/6054.pdf

Save the Children. (2013). *Alternative care in emergencies toolkit.* London: Author. www.unicef.org/protection/files/ace_toolkit_.pdf

Schwartz-Kenney, B. M., McCauley, M., & Epstein, M. A. (Eds.). (2000). *Child abuse: A global view.* Greenwood Press.

Sigelman, C. K., & Rider, E. A. (2006). *Life-span human development* (5th ed.). Thomson.

Special Representative of the Secretary General on Violence against Children. (2013). *Toward a world free from violence: Global survey on violence against children.* https://violenceagainstchildren.un.org/sites/violenceagainstchil dren.un.org/files/documents/publications/towards_a_world_free_from_vio lence_global_survey_low_res_fa.pdf

SOS-Kinderdorf International. (2008). *A child's 'right to a family': Family-based childcare: The experience, learning and vision of SOS Children's Villages: Position paper.* www.sos-childrensvillages.org/getmedia/cfe77e1e-45e0-4585-9e76-72066d4a03cc/ChildsRighttoFamily.pdf?ext=.pdf

Thomas, Jr, M. P. (1972). Child abuse and neglect: Part I – Historical overview, legal matrix, and social perspectives. *North Carolina Law Review,* 50(2). http://scholarship.law.unc.edu/nclr/vol50/iss2/3

Truong, T. D. (2001). *Human trafficking and organised crime.* www.research gate.net/publication/5130620_Human_trafficking_and_organised_crime

United Nations [UNCRC]. (1989). *Convention on the Rights of the Child.* www .ohchr.org/english/law/pdf/crc.pdf

United Nations. (2000). *Protocol to Prevent, Suppress and Punish Trafficking in Persons Especially Women and Children.* www.ohchr.org/en/professionalin terest/pages/protocoltraffickinginpersons.aspx

United Nations. (2005). *Guidelines on justice in matters involving child victims and witnesses of crime.* www.un.org/ruleoflaw/files/UNGuidelinesChildVictims Witnesses.pdf

United Nations. (2010). *Guidelines for the alternative care of children.* www .unicef.org/protection/alternative_care_Guidelines-English.pdf

United Nations. (2014). *Preventing and eliminating child, early and forced marriage.* https://documents-dds-ny.un.org/doc/UNDOC/GEN/G14/128/76/ PDF/G1412876.pdf?OpenElement

United Nations Children's Fund. (2004). *Child protection: A handbook for parliamentarians.* www.unicef.org/publications/index_21133.html

United Nations Children's Fund. (2006). *1946–2006: Sixty years for children: A State of the World's Children Special Report.* www.unicef.org/publications/ files/1946-2006_Sixty_Years_for_Children.pdf

United Nations Children's Fund. (2009). *Children and conflict in a changing world: Machel study 10-year strategic review.* https://childrenandarmed conflict.un.org/publications/MachelStudy-10YearStrategicReview_en .pdf

United Nations Children's Fund. (2011). Guidance for legislative reform on juvenile justice. Author. www.unicef.org/policyanalysis/files/Juvenile_justice _16052011_final.pdf

United Nations Children's Fund. (2015). *Teaching and learning about child rights.* www.unicef.org/crc/index_30184.html

United Nations Children's Fund. (2018). *A practical guide for developing child friendly spaces.* www.unicef.org/protection/A_Practical_Guide_to_Developing _Child_Friendly_Spaces_-_UNICEF_(1).pdf

United Nations Children's Fund. (2017). *A familiar face: Violence in the lives of children and adolescents.* New York. file:///C:/Users/murli/Downloads/ EVAC-Booklet-FINAL-10_31_17-high-res.pdf

United Nations Children's Fund and the Global Coalition to End Child Poverty. (2017). *A world free from child poverty.* New York. https://sustai nabledevelopment.un.org/index.php?page=view&type=400&nr=2434&menu =1515

United Nations ECOSOC (2002). Resolution 2002/12. *Basic principles on the use of restorative justice programmes in criminal matters.* www.un.org/en/ ecosoc/docs/2002/resolution%202002-12.pdf

United Nations General Assembly. (2007). UN *General Assembly adopts powerful definition of child poverty.* www.unicef.org/media/media_38003 .html

United Nations Office on Drugs and Crime. (2008). *Toolkit to Combat Trafficking in Persons.* www.unodc.org/res/cld/bibliography/toolkit-to-combat-traffick ing-in-persons_html/07-89375_Ebook1.pdf

United Nations Research Institute for Social Development [UNRISD]. (2010). *Combating poverty and inequality: Structural change, social policy and politics.* Geneva: Author. www.unrisd.org/publications/cpi

White, B. (2003). *A world fit for children? Dies Natalis Address delivered on the occasion of the 51st anniversary of the Institute of Social Studies*, The Hague, The Netherlands. http://lcms.eur.nl/iss/diesnatalis2003_ WhiteOCR.pdf

The World Bank. (2006). *World Development Report 2007: Development and the next generation.* Washington, DC: Author. www-wds.worldbank.org/ external/default/WDSContentServer/IW3P/IB/2006/09/13/000112742_200 60913111024/Rendered/PDF/359990WDR0complete.pdf

World Health Organization (2018). *INSPIRE Handbook: action for implementing the seven strategies for ending violence against children.* Geneva. www.who.int/publications/i/item/inspire-handbook-action-for-implementing-the-seven-strategies-for-ending-violence-against-children

World Health Organization [WHO]. (2020). *Global status report on preventing violence against children 2020.* file:///C:/Users/murli/Downloads/97892400 06379-eng%20(1).pdf

World Health Organization, Wartrauma Foundation, & World Vision. (2011). *Psychological first aid: Guide for field workers.* http://whqlibdoc.who.int/publications/2011/9789241548205_eng.pdf

Wyness, M. (2012). *Childhood and Society* (2nd ed.). Palgrave Macmillan.

Wyness, M., Harrison, L., & Buchanan, I. (2004). Childhood, politics and ambiguity: Towards an agenda for children's political inclusion. *Sociology, 38*(1), 81–99.

Acknowledgement

This Element is condensed, adapted from, and built on chapters of the following book by the author: Desai, M. (2019). *Rights-based integrated service delivery systems for child protection: Secondary and tertiary prevention*, A CRY Series of Sourcebooks on *Rights-Based Direct Practice with Children* by Springer Nature.

About the Author

Dr. Murli Desai obtained her master's degree in Social Work from the Tata Institute of Social Sciences (TISS), Mumbai, India, and doctoral degree in Social Work from Washington University in St. Louis, USA. After working for practice-based research in the field for four years, she was a faculty member at the TISS for the major part of her career, where the varied positions she held were Head of Unit for Family Studies, Head of Social Work Education and Practice Cell, and Associate Editor of The Indian Journal of Social Work. She subsequently worked at the Departments of Social Work at the National University of Singapore and at the Seoul National University.

She coordinated the national celebrations of the International Year of the Family, by Ministry of Welfare and TISS, sponsored by UNICEF, which led to preparation of India's approach paper on family policy. The Government of India bodies that she consulted with comprise Ministry of Women and Child Development and Indian Council for Child Welfare. The international systems that she provided consultation to include the UN Child Protection Working Group, and India offices of UNICEF and Save the Children. At the state level, she consulted with UNICEF Tamil Nadu and UNICEF Maharashtra. She contributed to field development through voluntary organisations such as Butterflies, Child Rights in Goa, and Child Rights and You. Among a total of nine books that she has authored, in 2018–19, she authored four sourcebooks for a CRY Series of Sourcebooks on Rights-Based Direct Practice with Children published by Springer Nature.

Cambridge Elements

Child Development

Marc H. Bornstein

National Institute of Child Health and Human Development, Bethesda
Institute for Fiscal Studies, London
UNICEF, New York City

Marc H. Bornstein is an Affiliate of the *Eunice Kennedy Shriver* National Institute of Child Health and Human Development, an International Research Fellow at the Institute for Fiscal Studies (London), and UNICEF Senior Advisor for Research for ECD Parenting Programmes. Bornstein is President Emeritus of the Society for Research in Child Development, Editor Emeritus of *Child Development*, and founding Editor of *Parenting: Science and Practice*.

About the Series

Child development is a lively and engaging, yet serious and purposeful subject of academic study that encompasses myriad of theories, methods, substantive areas, and applied concerns. Cambridge Elements in Child Development proposes to address all these key areas, with unique, comprehensive, and state-of-the-art treatments, introducing readers to the primary currents of research and to original perspectives on, or contributions to, principal issues and domains in the field.

Cambridge Elements ⲷ

Child Development

Elements in the Series

Child Development in Evolutionary Perspective
David F. Bjorklund

Gender in Childhood
Christia Spears Brown, Sharla D. Biefeld and Michelle J. Tam

The Child's Environment
Robert H. Bradley

The Nature of Intelligence and Its Development in Childhood
Robert J. Sternberg

Child Welfare, Protection, and Justice
Murli Desai

A full series listing is available at: www.cambridge.org/EICD

Printed in the United States
by Baker & Taylor Publisher Services